LUKE DIXON

Luke Dixon is a director, teacher and academic. He is internationally known for both productions of Shakespeare and site-specific work. He has directed and led workshops on Shakespeare around the world, from *A Midsummer Night's Dream* in Brazil to *Macbeth* in Hong Kong via *Pericles* in South Africa.

Luke is Artistic Director of Theatre Nomad and a regular tutor at London's Actors Centre. He is author of *Play-Acting: A Guide to Theatre Workshops*. For more information, see www.lukedixon.co.uk

THE GOOD AUDITION GUIDES

CLASSICAL MONOLOGUES
edited by Marina Caldarone

SHAKESPEARE MONOLOGUES
edited by Luke Dixon

SHAKESPEARE MONOLOGUES FOR YOUNG PEOPLE
edited by Luke Dixon

MODERN MONOLOGUES
edited by Trilby James

The Good Audition Guides

SHAKESPEARE MONOLOGUES FOR WOMEN

edited and introduced by
LUKE DIXON

NICK HERN BOOKS
London
www.nickhernbooks.co.uk

A NICK HERN BOOK

The Good Audition Guides:
Shakespeare Monologues for Women
first published in Great Britain in 2009
by Nick Hern Books Limited
The Glasshouse, 49a Goldhawk Road, London W12 8QP

Reprinted 2010, 2011, 2012, 2013

Cover design: www.energydesignstudio.com

Typeset by Country Setting, Kingsdown, Kent, CT14 8ES
Printed and bound in Great Britain by Mimeo Ltd, Huntingdon,
Cambs, PE29 6XX

A CIP catalogue record for this book
is available from the British Library

ISBN 978 1 84842 007 6

Contents

6

THE TRAGEDIES

Introduction

WHY SHAKESPEARE? ☞

The basic requirements for most auditions, from drama-school entry to a season at the recreated Globe Theatre in London, will include performing a speech by Shakespeare. Faced with the thirty-eight plays that are generally considered to have been written by Shakespeare, it is daunting for even the most experienced actor to know where to begin finding a suitable speech. Thirty-six of those plays were collected after Shakespeare's death by his colleagues and printed in what is known as the First Folio, a folio being the size of the sheet of paper it was printed on. Around 750 copies were produced and they sold for £1 each. About 230 still exist and now sell for around £3 million each. A couple of other plays only appeared in what are known as quarto editions, on paper folded to half the size of a folio sheet.

The Shakespearean canon, all the plays he wrote which have survived, is the heart of English drama. A speech from one of those plays can provide an actor with opportunities to show off their skills and talent in a whole range of ways: vocally and physically, in terms of characterisation and storytelling, emotionally and intellectually. A speech by Shakespeare is the best tool for an actor to demonstrate their craft, and for an audition panel or director to appreciate and judge it.

CHOOSING YOUR MONOLOGUE ☞

In this volume I have brought together fifty speeches, from some of the best known to the least common. You will never find a 'new' Shakespeare speech. Fashion and contemporary performance are factors that can make speeches appear current and popular. It is also best not to second-guess what speech the actor before or after you will perform. Best to find a speech that you like, enjoy performing and can in some way empathise with. Do not worry about what other actors are doing.

Choose more than one speech (maybe one comedy, one history and one tragedy) to have in your repertoire so that you always have something suitable when the call comes. Having chosen a speech, you *must* read the play and find the backstory so you know where the character and the speech are coming from.

Complexity   Some of the speeches in this book are relatively simple and might be more useful for the actor for whom Shakespeare is a new and terrifying experience: Miranda in *The Tempest* and Joan la Pucelle in *Henry VI, Part One*, perhaps fall into this category. Others, like Lady Macbeth and Helena in *All's Well That Ends Well*, are rich and complex in their language, thought and emotion and might be more suitable for actors seeking a challenge or needing to show the full range of their abilities.

Age   It is rare that we know the age of a character in a play by Shakespeare. Juliet we are told is fourteen. Otherwise ages are for the most part relative. The Countess in *All's Well That Ends Well* is older than Helena, whom she has just taken into her care. Lady Macbeth tells us that she has once 'given suck' to a child, which implies both age and a backstory that Shakespeare does not reveal in his play. In a production the director will make decisions about the age of his characters and their relative ages to each other, and may ask you to approximate a particular age. In an audition you can be much more flexible in deciding whether the speech of a character is suited to you and your playing age. To give you some guidance I have listed below 'younger' and 'older' characters whose speeches are in this book. I have done the same with status ('higher' and 'lower') and with lists of mothers and daughters (another indicator of age and status). I have also identified the speeches with the most obvious comic potential.

Gender   None of these speeches were written to be acted by a woman. Actresses did not exist in Shakespeare's theatre, and all the plays were written to be acted by men and boys. Gender and the dissemblance of gender are important themes through many of the plays. There are speeches here, both comic and serious, which give you plenty of opportunity to play with gender, from Joan la Pucelle in *Henry VI, Part One*, to Viola in *Twelfth Night* and Imogen in *Cymbeline*. I have included Rosalind's epilogue speech from *As You Like It* in which the gender of the actor is confused not for the other characters in the play but for the audience itself.

Length   The speeches vary considerably in the number of words, but not necessarily in the time they take to perform. Hermia's short speech in *A Midsummer Night's Dream*, when she wakens lost in the woods, though short of words, contains a great deal of implied action, and the action becomes as important as the words when you are performing it. It is a speech that needs to be given space to breathe and for the spaces and silences within it to be found. Cressida also has comparatively few words, yet her awkwardness and uncertainty means it takes what seems to her an eternity to deliver. In these and many other speeches there are important moments when the character is listening (Imogen in *Cymbeline* before she enters the cave) or when she is waiting for or expecting a reply (Portia in *Julius Caesar* and Marina in *Pericles*).

Where some speeches are too long for audition purposes I have, as judiciously as possible, made cuts.

LANGUAGE ☞

Shakespeare's audiences went to 'hear' plays. It was not until long after his death that anyone wrote of going to 'see' a play. So the sounds of Shakespeare's words are as important as their meanings. Indeed they often help convey the meanings. Enjoy and play with the sounds as you work through the speeches.

Prose is everyday speech but Shakespeare often heightens that speech, giving it colour, richness, images and so on that we would not use in our everyday lives.

Poetry is where that heightened use of language is taken further and the speech goes beyond the everyday, and rhythm and rhyme become important.

Verse is poetry where the rhythms of the words are organised.

Iambic pentameter is a particular kind of verse. An 'iamb' is where a short syllable is followed by a long syllable giving a 'di-dum' rhythm. 'Metre' is how rhythms are organised in lines of verse. 'Penta' is the old Greek word for five. So if you put five iambs in a line of verse you get an iambic pentameter:

di-dum, di-dum, di-dum, di-dum, di-dum

This was the main form Shakespeare used in writing his plays: they are the heartbeat of his language. Sometimes it is used rigidly and is easy to spot:

How happy some o'er other some can be!
Through Athens I am thought as fair as she.
(Helena, *A Midsummer Night's Dream*)

Sometimes, especially as he got older and more experienced, Shakespeare played with the form and pulled it around for emotional, dramatic or characterisation effect.

In order for the rhythm to work, a word ending in '–ed' will sometimes have the letters stressed as a syllable, in which case it is printed '–èd', and sometimes it will not be a separate syllable but be spoken as if the 'e' is not there, in which case it is printed '–'d'.

Rhyming couplets   Sometimes Shakespeare uses rhyme and when two lines together rhyme we have a rhyming couplet. Often these are used at the end of a speech or scene to indicate finality.

Punctuation in Shakespeare is a controversial subject. Shakespeare did not prepare his plays for publication and therefore the punctuation in the texts is largely put there by his colleagues or the publisher or printer. Nonetheless, the punctuation in the speeches I have chosen, which follow for the most part the First Folio, can give you some help not just with sense but also with where to breathe, pause, rest, change gear or change thought.

Vocabulary   Shakespeare wrote at a time when English as we know it was developing rapidly. He made up or used for the first time many words and phrases that are now part of our everyday speech. Words that were brand new when Shakespeare used them include: accommodation, critic, dwindle, eventful, exposure, frugal, generous, gloomy, laughable, majestic, misplaced, monumental, multitudinous and obscene. Phrases that he coined include: disgraceful conduct, elbow-room, fair play, green-eyed monster, method in his madness, to thine own self be true, the lady doth protest too much, and it's Greek to me. Some of the words he used or invented have faded from the language ('fadge' meaning 'to turn out' in Viola's speech from *Twelfth Night*, for example), and some words which are familiar today had different, stronger meanings then, than now. In both these cases, I have glosed their meanings in the notes.

THE AUDITION ☞

Thought process   It is rare that a character sets out to make a speech, though in some of the big public and political scenes a character does just that. Hermione in *The Winter's Tale* has come prepared to defend herself before her accuser, and Portia, too, in *The Merchant of Venice* has a speech to make in court. But for the most part a speech starts with a single thought which is followed by another and then another until the character has said enough – or been interrupted. Allow time for each of those thoughts to come and be fresh in the mind before they are spoken. Do not be daunted by what can seem endless lines of text. It is not a race to get through to the end. Take the speech one thought at a time.

Structure   As you follow the thoughts, follow too the emotions and language of the speech. Look for its structure. Let yourself show the full range of emotion and vocal possibility within the speech. Seek variety. None of these speeches is on one note. All allow a wide range of vocal and emotional expression.

Setting and geography   Many of these speeches are soliloquies allowing the character to express her thoughts or ideas to an audience while she is alone, such as Viola in *Twelfth Night*. Other speeches, like Goneril's in *King Lear*, are parts of dialogues or conversations. And some, such as Paulina's in *The Winter's Tale*, are directed to large public gatherings. Others may be a combination of all these. Decide who else, if anyone, is there to hear the speech and where they are placed. Give thought to the geography or layout of the place the speech is being spoken in – whether the woods of *A Midsummer Night's Dream*, the palace of Cleopatra, or the windswept island of *The Tempest*. Take a few moments when you first come into the audition room to place the other characters and recreate the geography and setting in your mind's eye (another phrase Shakespeare coined).

Audience   If your speech is directed to an audience, it can be a theatre audience or an audience within the scene. Some speeches are soliloquies which can be played to oneself, to the audience or some combination of the two (Viola and Olivia in *Twelfth Night*). Others are to a public audience within the play (Hermione and Paulina in *The Winter's Tale*). Decide whether and how to use your audition panel as that audience.

Make the space your own   Many other actors will have been in the audition room before you. Many will come after you. Spend a moment or two before you start your speech by focusing and allowing the panel to focus on you. Create the silence out of which your words will come and decide on the energy that the words will bring with them, whether the distress and anguish of Miranda in *The Tempest* shouting across the storm, or Lady Macbeth preparing to summon up spirits in what might be a fearful silence.

HOW TO USE THIS BOOK ☞

For each speech I have given an indication of:

WHERE ☞   If possible I have indicated where and when the action is taking place. Sometimes this can be very specific, either because Shakespeare has told us or because the action is tied to a particular historical event. If the plays are set in times of legend or myth, the date and place are of no direct importance in affecting how you perform them.

WHO ELSE IS THERE ☞   This note gives an indication of who else is on stage and the character's relationship to them.

WHAT IS HAPPENING ☞   This note will give a context for the speech but it is not a substitute for reading the play and yourself deciding where the speech is coming from.

WHAT TO THINK ABOUT ☞   I have indicated some ideas of things to think about as you are working on the speech. This is by no means an exhaustive list but will give you a way into the speech and should spark other thoughts and ideas of your own.

WHERE ELSE TO LOOK ☞   If you like a speech or character and want to look elsewhere in this collection for similar pieces, this will help you on your way.

GLOSSARY ☞   I have glossed the trickier and more perplexing words, phrases and thoughts in the speeches, but do not worry if you need a dictionary or annotated edition of the play to help you fully understand what your character is saying.

THE TEXTS ☞   Wherever possible, I have used the exemplary texts of *The Shakespeare Folios* published by Nick Hern Books and edited by Nick de Somogyi, and the speeches appear in the order that they do in the First Folio (comedies, then histories, then tragedies). Speeches from plays not yet published in this series have been edited by me from the First Folio using the same editorial rules. In the case of *Pericles* and *The Two Noble Kinsmen*, neither of which appears in the First Folio and both of which are of contested authorship, I have used Quarto texts edited in the same way. All the glosses are my own.

The following categories may help you find a particular attribute that suits you, or your monologue:

- OLDER

  The Countess of Rossillion in *All's Well That Ends Well*
  Olivia in *Twelfth Night*
  Hermione in *The Winter's Tale*
  Paulina in *The Winter's Tale*
  Lady Constance in *King John*
  Duchess of Gloucester in *Richard II*
  The Hostess in *Henry V*
  Duchess of Gloucester in *Henry VI, Part Two*
  Queen Margaret in *Henry VI, Part Two*
  Queen Katharine in *Henry VIII*
  Volumnia in *Coriolanus*
  The Nurse in *Romeo and Juliet*
  Emilia in *Othello*
  Cleopatra in *Antony and Cleopatra*

- YOUNGER

  Miranda in *The Tempest*
  Isabella in *Measure for Measure*
  The Princess of France in *Love's Labour's Lost*
  Helena in *A Midsummer Night's Dream*
  Hermia in *A Midsummer Night's Dream*
  Jessica in *The Merchant of Venice*
  Portia in *The Merchant of Venice*
  Phoebe in *As You Like It*
  Rosalind in *As You Like It*
  Helena in *All's Well That Ends Well*
  Viola in *Twelfth Night*
  Joan la Pucelle in *Henry VI, Part One*
  Cressida in *Troilus and Cressida*
  Ophelia in *Hamlet*
  Desdemona in *Othello*
  The Jailer's Daughter in *The Two Noble Kinsmen*

- MOTHERS

  The Countess of Rossillion in *All's Well That Ends Well*
  Lady Constance in *King John*

- DAUGHTERS

  Miranda in *The Tempest*
  Jessica in *The Merchant of Venice*
  Marina in *Pericles*
  Juliet in *Romeo and Juliet*
  Ophelia in *Hamlet*
  The Jailer's Daughter in *The Two Noble Kinsmen*

- HIGHER STATUS

  The Princess of France in *Love's Labour's Lost*
  Portia in *The Merchant of Venice*
  Olivia in *Twelfth Night*
  Hermione in *The Winter's Tale*
  Queen Margaret in *Henry VI, Part Three*
  Volumnia in *Coriolanus*
  Lady Macbeth in *Macbeth*
  Cleopatra in *Antony and Cleopatra*

- LOWER STATUS

  Phoebe in *As You Like It*
  Paulina in *The Winter's Tale*
  The Hostess in *Henry V*
  The Nurse in *Romeo and Juliet*
  The Jailer's Daughter in *The Two Noble Kinsmen*

- COMIC

  Luciana in *The Comedy of Errors*
  Phoebe in *As You Like It*
  The Hostess in *Henry V*
  The Nurse in *Romeo and Juliet*

The Comedies

The Tempest

WHO ☞ *Miranda, a young girl.*

WHERE ☞ *Somewhere on Prospero's island.*

WHO ELSE IS THERE ☞ *The magician Prospero, Miranda's father.*

WHAT IS HAPPENING ☞ *A tempest has wrecked a ship on the coast of the island on which Miranda lives with her father. Having watched the ship go down, Miranda pleads with her father that, if he is responsible for the tempest, he must stop it.*

WHAT TO THINK ABOUT ☞

- *Decide if Miranda has any fear of her father and how courageous she might have to be to stand up to him.*
- *Imagine the images of the sinking ship and their impact on Miranda.*
- *Decide how far from the sea Miranda has run to find her father and how out of breath she might be.*
- *The suffering she has seen will affect her speech and behaviour.*
- *Decide whether the storm she describes has abated or whether it is still visible or even raging around or close by.*

WHERE ELSE TO LOOK ☞ *Another daughter pleading with her father is Marina (Pericles, p. 60).*

Miranda

" If by your art, my dearest father, you have
Put the wild waters in this roar, allay them.
The sky, it seems, would pour down stinking pitch,
But that the sea, mounting to th' welkin's cheek,*
Dashes the fire out. O! I have suffer'd
With those that I saw suffer. A brave vessel
(Who had no doubt some noble creature in her)
Dash'd all to pieces. O! the cry did knock
Against my very heart. Poor souls, they perish'd.
Had I been any god of power, I would
Have sunk the sea within the earth or ere*
It should the good ship so have swallow'd, and
The fraughting souls* within her. **"**

(*Act 1, scene 2, lines 1–13*)

GLOSSARY

welkin's cheek – the edge of the sky
or ere – before
fraughting souls – passengers (fraughting means freight-ing rather than
    fright-ing)

Measure for Measure

WHO ☞ *Isabella, a novice in a nunnery.*

WHERE ☞ *A room in the palace in Vienna.*

WHO ELSE IS THERE ☞ *Isabella is alone.*

WHAT IS HAPPENING ☞ *Angelo, who is ruling Vienna in the Duke's absence, has told Isabella he will halt the execution of her brother if she will offer up her virginity to him. Alone on stage she realises no one will believe her if she tells what he has said.*

WHAT TO THINK ABOUT ☞

- *Imagine how high the stakes are as Isabella has to choose between giving Angelo her virginity and saving her brother's life.*

- *Think how lonely she must feel at the beginning of the speech.*

- *Decide why she trusts nobody and thinks no one will believe her story.*

- *Decide what it is about her relationship with her brother that makes her think he would have his head chopped off twenty times for her sake.*

- *Isabella remembers telling Angelo that her chastity is more important to her than her brother's life and she paraphrases the words she said to him: 'More than our brother is our chastity'. Decide why her chastity is so important to her.*

- *Her brother has been condemned to death for having sex outside of marriage; Angelo has demanded sex with Isabella to save him. Think how this might affect Isabella's feelings about men and sex.*

WHERE ELSE TO LOOK ☞ *Another young woman desperate for help is Desdemona (Othello, p. 112).*

Isabella

❝ To whom should I complain? Did I tell this,
Who would believe me? O perilous mouths
That bear in them one and the selfsame tongue,
Either of condemnation or approof;*
Bidding the law make curtsy to their will,
Hooking both right and wrong to th'appetite,
To follow as it draws! I'll to my brother.
Though he hath fallen by prompture of the blood,*
Yet hath he in him such a mind of honour
That had he twenty heads to tender down
On twenty bloody blocks, he'd yield them up
Before his sister should her body stoop
To such abhorr'd pollution.
Then Isabel live chaste, and brother die:
'More than our brother is our chastity.'
I'll tell him yet of Angelo's request,
And fit his mind to death, for his soul's rest. ❞

(*Act 2, scene 4, lines 171–87*)

GLOSSARY

approof – approval
by prompture of the blood – because he gave in to his urges

The Comedy of Errors

WHO ☞ *Luciana, sister-in-law of Antipholus of Ephesus.*

WHERE ☞ *Before the house of Antipholus of Ephesus.*

WHO ELSE IS THERE ☞ *The Antipholus who comes from Syracuse, but who Luciana believes to be her sister's husband.*

WHAT IS HAPPENING ☞ *There is confusion between identical twin brothers, both named Antipholus. Luciana mistakenly believes that the Antipholus she is haranguing has been unfaithful to his wife, her sister Adriana, and here urges him to be a more careful adulterer.*

WHAT TO THINK ABOUT ☞

- *She begins by being cross with Antipholus but then her tone changes and she gives him advice on how to misbehave without getting caught.*
- *Decide where Luciana has learnt the tricks of successful sexual deceit.*
- *Perhaps her sister is close by and within hearing.*
- *Decide how attractive Antipholus might be to Luciana.*
- *Luciana starts by calling Antipholus 'you' but then changes to the more familiar and intimate 'thy' and through the speech vacillates between the two.*
- *The speech is written in alternating rhymes. Think about how the formal quality affects the tone of what Luciana has to say.*

WHERE ELSE TO LOOK ☞ *Women despairing in their different ways of their husbands' behaviour are Emilia (Othello, p. 114) and the Duchess of Gloucester (Henry VI, Part Two, p. 76).*

Luciana

" And may it be that you have quite forgot
A husband's office? Shall, Antipholus,
Even in the spring of love, thy love-springs rot?
Shall love in building* grow so ruinous?
If you did wed my sister for her wealth,
Then for her wealth's sake use her with more kindness.
Or if you like elsewhere do it by stealth,
Muffle your false love with some show of blindness.
Let not my sister read it in your eye.
Be not thy tongue thy own shame's orator.
Look sweet, speak fair, become disloyalty.
Apparel vice like virtue's harbinger.*
Bear a fair presence, though your heart be tainted,
Teach sin the carriage of a holy saint,
Be secret-false: what need she be acquainted?
What simple thief brags of his own attaint?
'Tis double wrong, to truant with your bed,
And let her read it in thy looks at board.*
Shame hath a bastard fame, well managèd;
Ill deeds are doubled with an evil word.
Alas, poor women! Make us but believe
(Being compact of credit)* that you love us;
Though others have the arm, show us the sleeve.
We in your motion turn and you may move us.
Then, gentle brother, get you in again;
Comfort my sister, cheer her, call her wife;
'Tis holy sport to be a little vain
When the sweet breath of flattery conquers strife. **"**

(*Act 3, scene 2, lines 1–28*)

GLOSSARY

in building – while being constructed
apparel vice like virtue's harbinger – dress up vice like the herald of
   virtue
board – mealtimes
compact of credit – credulous, easily deceived

Love's Labour's Lost

WHO ☞ *The Princess of France.*

WHERE ☞ *Navarre, now in north-east Spain, then an independent kingdom.*

WHO ELSE IS THERE ☞ *The King of Navarre, Lords and Ladies, a clown and others.*

WHAT IS HAPPENING ☞ *Ferdinand, the King of Navarre, asks for the heart and hand of the Princess, but having earlier been deceived by him she will not give it straight away. She tells him that if he comes back after going away and living in a monastery for a year, then she will marry him.*

WHAT TO THINK ABOUT ☞

- *The Princess has just been told of the death of her father and that she is now Queen of France. She is grieving as Ferdinand asks her to marry him.*

- *Decide when and why she comes up with the idea of sending him away for a year.*

- *This is a very public scene and the Princess has just become Queen, two things which might affect her conduct.*

- *She touches Ferdinand's palm with her palm ('by this virgin palm, now kissing thine') and holds it there as she waits for his response, a moment both public and intimate.*

WHERE ELSE TO LOOK ☞ *Other young women caught between grief for their fathers and new found loves include Helena (All's Well That Ends Well, p. 46) and Jessica (The Merchant of Venice, p. 32).*

Princess

66 No, no, my lord, your grace is perjur'd much,
Full of dear guiltiness, and therefore this:
If for my love (as there is no such cause)
You will do aught, this shall you do for me.
Your oath I will not trust. But go with speed
To some forlorn and naked hermitage,*
Remote from all the pleasures of the world.
There stay, until the twelve celestial signs*
Have brought about the annual reckoning.
If this austere insociable life
Change not your offer made in heat of blood;
If frosts, and fasts, hard lodging, and thin weeds*
Nip not the gaudy blossoms of your love,
But that it bear this trial, and last love;
Then at the expiration of the year,
Come challenge me, challenge me by these deserts,
And, by this virgin palm, now kissing thine,
I will be thine. And till that instant shut
My woeful self up in a mourning house,
Raining the tears of lamentation
For the remembrance of my father's death.
If this thou do deny, let our hands part,
Neither entitled in the other's heart. **99**

(Act 5, scene 2, lines 783–805)

GLOSSARY

naked hermitage – austere monastery
twelve celestial signs – twelve signs of the zodiac, i.e. a whole year
thin weeds – flimsy clothes

A Midsummer Night's Dream

WHO ☞ *Helena, a young Athenian woman.*

WHERE ☞ *The court in Athens.*

WHO ELSE IS THERE ☞ *Helena is alone.*

WHAT IS HAPPENING ☞ *Helena loves Demetrius, who in turn loves her best friend Hermia. Left alone by her friends, Helena bemoans the injustices of love.*

WHAT TO THINK ABOUT ☞

- *Helena is deeply in love with Demetrius, but he loves her best friend Hermia. Decide how this might affect the ways in which she speaks both their names.*

- *She thinks about Cupid the God of Love and realises why he is always represented as being blind. Decide whether she has thought of this previously or whether this is a new thought.*

- *Decide whether Helena has ever been in love before.*

- *Think how the idea to tell Demetrius about Hermia running away comes to her.*

- *The speech is written in rhyming couplets, which usually result in strongly end-stopped lines. Decide whether these should be emphasised and when – and why – they should be run on.*

WHERE ELSE TO LOOK ☞ *Another Helena (All's Well That Ends Well, p. 46) is also spurned by the man she loves.*

Helena

" How happy some o'er other some can be!
Through Athens I am thought as fair as she.
But what of that? Demetrius thinks not so.
He will not know what all but he do know,
And as he errs, doting on Hermia's eyes,
So I, admiring of his qualities.
Things base and vile, holding no quantity,*
Love can transpose to form and dignity.
Love looks not with the eyes, but with the mind,
And therefore is wing'd Cupid painted blind.
Nor hath Love's mind of any judgement taste.
Wings and no eyes figure unheedy haste.*
And therefore is Love said to be a child,
Because in choice he is so oft beguil'd.
As waggish* boys in game themselves forswear,
So the boy Love is perjur'd everywhere.
For ere Demetrius look'd on Hermia's eyne,*
He hail'd down oaths that he was only mine.
And when this hail some heat from Hermia felt,
So he dissolv'd, and showers of oaths did melt.
I will go tell him of fair Hermia's flight:
Then to the wood will he tomorrow night
Pursue her; and for this intelligence
If I have thanks, it is a dear expense.
But herein mean I to enrich my pain,
To have his sight thither and back again. **"**

(Act 1, scene 1, lines 226–51)

GLOSSARY

holding no quantity – with no intrinsic value
figure unheedy haste – symbolise reckless haste
waggish – mischievous
eyne – eyes

A Midsummer Night's Dream

WHO ☞ *Hermia, a young Athenian woman.*

WHERE ☞ *The woods outside Athens, early morning.*

WHO ELSE IS THERE ☞ *Hermia is alone.*

WHAT IS HAPPENING ☞ *Eloping into the woods with her lover Lysander, Hermia has fallen asleep. Wakened by a bad dream she realises that Lysander is nowhere to be found.*

WHAT TO THINK ABOUT ☞

- *This is a whole scene. Hermia is asleep at the beginning, wakes dreaming, looks for her lover, realises he is gone, wonders what to do, and decides to look for him. Give it the time and space it needs.*

- *Decide at what point she is fully awake and how she feels when she realises she has been dreaming.*

- *Work out the geography of the scene. Decide where Lysander went to sleep and what the woods around Hermia are like.*

- *Imagine what it would be like to wake up in the woods if you have never slept in the open air before.*

- *Decide how loudly Hermia has to shout before she realises Lysander cannot hear her.*

- *Imagine how scary it could be to go off alone into the trees to find death or your lover.*

- *Think about how the rhyming couplets might affect the tone of the scene.*

WHERE ELSE TO LOOK ☞ *Imogen (Cymbeline, p. 120) is also on her own in the open air a long way from home.*

Hermia

Awaking.

❝ Help me, Lysander, help me; do thy best
To pluck this crawling serpent from my breast!
Ay me, for pity; what a dream was here?
Lysander, look how I do quake with fear.
Methought a serpent eat my heart away,
And you sat smiling at his cruel prey.
Lysander, what, remov'd? Lysander, lord,
What, out of hearing, gone? No sound, no word?
Alack, where are you? Speak, and if you hear,
Speak, of all loves! I swoon almost with fear.
No? Then I well perceive you are not nigh.
Either death or you I'll find immediately. **❞**

(Act 2, scene 2, lines 145–56)

The Merchant of Venice

WHO ☞ *Jessica, daughter of Shylock a Jewish money-lender.*

WHERE ☞ *Her father's house in Venice.*

WHO ELSE IS THERE ☞ *Launcelot, a clown, though he exits on the line 'Farewell, good Launcelot'.*

WHAT IS HAPPENING ☞ *Launcelot is leaving the employ of Jessica's father Shylock. Jessica herself is intending to elope that night with her lover Lorenzo. Here she says farewell to Launcelot and asks him secretly to take a letter to her lover.*

WHAT TO THINK ABOUT ☞

- *Jessica might be within earshot of her father or others in the house. Decide how this might affect the way in which she talks to Launcelot.*

- *Launcelot brings some lightness to the house and she enjoys his company.*

- *She gives Launcelot some money and then gives him a secret letter for her lover. Think how these might be done and whether both are done in the same way.*

- *Decide how differently she would speak the last six lines once she is alone.*

- *Decide how strong the guilt is she feels at the thought of leaving her father and what her feelings are about renouncing her Judaism and becoming a Christian.*

WHERE ELSE TO LOOK ☞ *Also torn between duty to their fathers and desire for the men they love are Portia (The Merchant of Venice, p. 34) and Helena (All's Well That Ends Well, p. 46).*

Jessica

" I am sorry thou wilt leave my father so,
Our house is hell, and thou a merry devil
Didst rob it of some taste of tediousness.
But fare thee well, there is a ducat for thee,
And Launcelot, soon at supper shalt thou see
Lorenzo, who is thy new master's guest;
Give him this letter, do it secretly,
And so farewell. I would not have my father
See me in talk with thee.
                   Farewell, good Launcelot.
Alack, what heinous sin is it in me
To be asham'd to be my father's child!
But though I am a daughter to his blood,
I am not to his manners. O Lorenzo,
If thou keep promise, I shall end this strife,
Become a Christian and thy loving wife. **"**

                      (Act 2, scene 3, lines 1–21)

The Merchant of Venice

WHO ☞ *Portia, an heiress.*

WHERE ☞ *A room in Portia's house on her estate near Venice.*

WHO ELSE IS THERE ☞ *Nerissa (her waiting-gentlewoman), Bassanio, and his friend Graziano, 'and all their trains'.*

WHAT IS HAPPENING ☞ *Portia is in love with Bassanio. Under the terms of her late father's will her suitors have to choose between three caskets. If Bassanio chooses the casket that has Portia's portrait inside he can marry her. Portia urges Bassanio to delay his choosing in case he makes the wrong choice.*

WHAT TO THINK ABOUT ☞

- *Portia wants to make time go slowly. First she asks Bassanio to wait a day or two and then a month or two.*

- *She is caught between the promise she made her father and her desire to tell Bassiano which casket to choose.*

- *There are other people present and she may not wish everyone to hear everything she says. Decide to whom she delivers each line.*

- *There may be some thoughts she does not want even Bassanio to hear.*

- *She says that 'it is not love' at first, then clearly admits her love as the speech goes on.*

- *'Naughty' would have been a much stronger word to Portia than it is to us, meaning evil or wicked.*

WHERE ELSE TO LOOK ☞ *Cressida (Troilus and Cressida, p. 88) admits to her love. Juliet (Romeo and Juliet, p. 100) wants time not to go more slowly but more quickly.*

Portia

❝ I pray you, tarry, pause a day or two
Before you hazard, for, in choosing wrong,
I lose your company; therefore forbear awhile,
There's something tells me (but it is not love)
I would not lose you, and you know yourself,
Hate counsels not in such a quality.*
But lest you should not understand me well –
And yet a maiden hath no tongue but thought –
I would detain you here some month or two
Before you venture for me. I could teach you
How to choose right, but I am then forsworn,*
So will I never be, so may you miss me,
But if you do, you'll make me wish a sin,
That I had been forsworn. Beshrew your eyes,
They have o'erlook'd me and divided me:
One half of me is yours, the other half yours,
Mine own I would say; but if mine then yours,
And so all yours.* O, these naughty times
Put bars between the owners and their rights!
And so though yours, not yours: prove it so,
Let fortune go to hell for it, not I.
I speak too long; but 'tis to peize* the time,
To eke it and to draw it out in length,
To stay you from election. **❞**

(Act 3, scene 2, lines 1–24)

GLOSSARY

in such a quality – in this manner
I am thus forsworn – I have then broken my promise
Beshrew your eyes . . . And so all yours – Portia is babbling (she curses
    Bassanio's eyes saying that they have cut her in half. But even the
    half that they have left to her is Bassanio's)
peize – weigh down, lessen the speed of

The Merchant of Venice

WHO ☞   *Portia, an heiress, dressed like a male doctor of law.*

WHERE ☞   *A court of justice, Venice.*

WHO ELSE IS THERE ☞   *Shylock, the Jewish money-lender, Antonio, the merchant (or businessman) of Venice who owes him money, Bassanio, Portia's fiancé, and many others.*

WHAT IS HAPPENING ☞   *Antonio has borrowed money from the Jewish money-lender Shylock on behalf of his friend Bassanio who wanted it to further his attempts to woo Portia. Antonio is unable to pay back the debt and Shylock is seeking the pound of Antonio's flesh that he was promised as security for the loan. Now engaged to Bassanio, Portia comes in disguise to the court to offer legal advice.*

WHAT TO THINK ABOUT ☞

- *Portia is in disguise. Decide how this will affect your (and her) performance.*

- *The speech is a public one, full of wisdom, which later becomes specific to the case.*

- *Think of her religious beliefs and her attitude to the Christian God she talks of.*

- *Think what her attitude might be to Shylock whom she just calls 'Jew'.*

- *The speech ends with the prospect of death for Antonio.*

WHERE ELSE TO LOOK ☞   *Other courtroom speeches are those of Hermione and Paulina (The Winter's Tale, pp. 54, 56 and 58).*

Portia

❝ The quality of mercy is not strain'd,*
It droppeth as the gentle rain from heaven
Upon the place beneath: it is twice blest;
It blesseth him that gives and him that takes:
'Tis mightiest in the mightiest: it becomes
The thronèd monarch better than his crown.
His sceptre shows the force of temporal* power,
The attribute to awe and majesty,
Wherein doth sit the dread and fear of kings.
But mercy is above this sceptred sway.
It is enthronèd in the hearts of kings,
It is an attribute to God himself.
And earthly power doth then show likest God's
When mercy seasons* justice. Therefore, Jew,
Though justice be thy plea, consider this:
That, in the course of justice, none of us
Should see salvation. We do pray for mercy;
And that same prayer doth teach us all to render
The deeds of mercy. I have spoke thus much
To mitigate the justice of thy plea,
Which if thou follow, this strict court of Venice
Must needs give sentence 'gainst the merchant there. **❞**

(*Act 4, scene 1, lines 184–205*)

GLOSSARY

strain'd – forced, constrained
temporal – earthly
seasons – modifies, sweetens, alleviates

As You Like It

WHO ☞   *Phoebe, a country girl.*

WHERE ☞   *The Forest of Arden, named after a forest of the same name in North Warwickshire, near Stratford.*

WHO ELSE IS THERE ☞   *Silvius, a young shepherd.*

WHAT IS HAPPENING ☞   *Silvius is heartbroken that Phoebe does not love him and has told her that a common executioner is more gentle than she is.*

WHAT TO THINK ABOUT ☞

- *Decide what Phoebe thinks of Silvius and the way in which he dotes on her.*

- *Phoebe is amazed that Silvius can think that the look in her eyes can kill him. She sarcastically agrees that this is 'pretty sure and very probable'! She frowns on him and challenges him to fall down if her look is wounding him. Maybe she waits for him to fall.*

- *Play with the possibilities of physical comedy in the scene as Phoebe tries to hurt Silvius with her looks.*

WHERE ELSE TO LOOK ☞   *Luciana (The Comedy of Errors, p. 24) is another woman taunting a man because of his love.*

Phoebe

" I would not be thy executioner:
I fly thee, for I would not injure thee.
Thou tell'st me there is murder in mine eye:
'Tis pretty sure, and very probable,
That eyes, that are the frail'st and softest things,
Who shut their coward gates on atomies,*
Should be call'd tyrants, butchers, murderers!
Now I do frown on thee with all my heart,
And if mine eyes can wound, now let them kill thee.
Now counterfeit to swoon, why, now fall down;
Or if thou canst not, O, for shame, for shame,
Lie not, to say mine eyes are murderers!
Now show the wound mine eye hath made in thee.
Scratch thee but with a pin, and there remains
Some scar of it; lean but upon a rush,*
The cicatrice* and capable impressure*
Thy palm some moment keeps. But now mine eyes,
Which I have darted at thee, hurt thee not,
Nor, I am sure, there is no force in eyes
That can do hurt. **"**

(Act 3, scene 5, lines 8–27)

GLOSSARY

atomies – specks
rush – reed, single straw
cicatrice – scar
capable impressure – sensitive imprint

As You Like It

WHO ☞ *Phoebe, a country girl.*

WHERE ☞ *The Forest of Arden, named after a forest of the same name in North Warwickshire, near Stratford.*

WHO ELSE IS THERE ☞ *Silvius, a young shepherd.*

WHAT IS HAPPENING ☞ *Silvius loves Phoebe but Phoebe is falling in love with 'Ganymede' (Rosalind in the disguise of a man). Phoebe denies that she is in love, but as she describes Ganymede to Silvius it is clear that she dotes on him.*

WHAT TO THINK ABOUT ☞

- *Remember that Silvius is in love with Phoebe.*

- *Decide whether Phoebe denies her love of Ganymede just to Silvius or to herself as well.*

- *She can get lost in her memories of her conversation with Ganymede and forget at times that Silvius is there.*

- *Decide what she thinks of herself as she remembers her part in the conversation.*

- *Decide how the idea of sending a letter to Ganymede comes about and what tone she takes with Silvius to persuade him to take the letter on her behalf.*

WHERE ELSE TO LOOK ☞ *Recalling a recent conversation and so realising she is in love is Olivia (Twelfth Night, p. 50).*

Phoebe

❝ Think not I love him, though I ask for him.
'Tis but a peevish boy; yet he talks well –
But what care I for words? Yet words do well
When he that speaks them pleases those that hear.
It is a pretty youth – not very pretty;
But sure he's proud – and yet his pride becomes him.
He'll make a proper* man; the best thing in him
Is his complexion; and faster than his tongue
Did make offence, his eye did heal it up.
He is not very tall – yet for his years he's tall.
His leg is but so-so – and yet 'tis well.
There was a pretty redness in his lip,
A little riper and more lusty red
Than that mix'd in his cheek; 'twas just the difference
Between the constant red and mingled damask.*
There be some women, Silvius, had they mark'd him
In parcels,* as I did, would have gone near
To fall in love with him. But for my part,
I love him not; nor hate him not; and yet
I have more cause to hate him than to love him:
For what had he to do to chide at me?
He said mine eyes were black, and my hair black,
And, now I am remember'd, scorn'd at me.
I marvel why I answer'd not again,
But that's all one. Omittance is no quittance.*
I'll write to him a very taunting letter,
And thou shalt bear it – wilt thou, Silvius? **❞**

(*Act 3, scene 5, lines 109–35*)

GLOSSARY

proper – handsome, attractive
constant red and mingled damask – the bright red and pink of different
    types of rose
mark'd him / In parcels – paid attention to each of his component parts
omittance is no quittance – just because I didn't say it doesn't mean I
    won't do it (a common saying)

As You Like It

WHO ☞ *Rosalind (or more properly, the actor/actress playing Rosalind).*

WHERE ☞ *The stage at the end of the play.*

WHO ELSE IS THERE ☞ *S/he is speaking to the audience.*

WHAT IS HAPPENING ☞ *Through most of the play Rosalind has been disguised as a man, causing sexual and romantic confusion. She comes forward at the end of the play and, as both man and woman, talks to the audience.*

WHAT TO THINK ABOUT ☞

- *This is an opportunity to be the actor (of either gender) and the male and female roles they have adopted.*

- *There is a great deal of flirting with the audience and much sexual innuendo.*

- *Rosalind conjures the audience and almost puts them under a spell. Conjure was a strong word in Shakespeare's time with connotations of witchcraft.*

WHERE ELSE TO LOOK ☞ *Viola (Twelfth Night, p. 52) also talks to the audience about the complexities and dangers of gender disguise. Joan la Pucelle (Henry VI, Part One, p. 74) virtually changes gender during her speech.*

Rosalind

" It is not the fashion to see the lady the Epilogue; but it is no more unhandsome than to see the lord the Prologue. If it be true that good wine needs no bush,* 'tis true that a good play needs no epilogue. Yet to good wine they do use good bushes, and good plays prove the better by the help of good epilogues. What a case am I in, then, that am neither a good epilogue nor cannot insinuate with you in the behalf of a good play? I am not furnished* like a beggar, therefore to beg will not become me. My way is to conjure you, and I'll begin with the women. I charge you, O women, for the love you bear to men, to like as much of this play as please you. And I charge you, O men, for the love you bear to women – as I perceive by your simpering, none of you hates them – that between you and the women, the play may please. If I were a woman, I would kiss as many of you as had beards that pleased me, complexions that liked me, and breaths that I defied not. And, I am sure, as many as have good beards, or good faces, or sweet breaths, will for my kind offer, when I make curtsy, bid me farewell. **"**

(*Epilogue*)

GLOSSARY

bush – advertisement (the ivy-bush of an inn-sign)
furnished – dressed

The Taming of the Shrew

WHO ☞ *Katharina.*

WHERE ☞ *A room in Lucentio's house in Padua.*

WHO ELSE IS THERE ☞ *Katharina's sister Bianca is getting married. Amongst the wedding party are the sisters' father Baptista and their respective husbands Petruchio and Lucentio.*

WHAT IS HAPPENING ☞ *Katharina had a reputation as being wilful and ungovernable (the 'shrew' of the play's title). Petruchio married her in the hope of 'taming' her. At her sister's wedding she surprises everyone by advising the other wives there to be submissive to their husbands.*

WHAT TO THINK ABOUT ☞

- *Katharina has a big audience of family and friends. Her husband is also there. Work out the geography of the scene and where the characters she is speaking to are situated.*

- *Plot which lines are directed at which people – her father, sister, husband.*

- *Decide whether what Katharina is saying is as much a revelation to her as it is to those around her.*

- *Decide how much of the speech is a declaration of love to her husband.*

- *Much of the speech may be a description of her own previous behaviour and therefore be spoken with remorse.*

WHERE ELSE TO LOOK ☞ *Emilia (Othello, p. 114) has a different view of male–female relations.*

Katharina

❝ Fie, fie! Unknit that threatening unkind brow,
And dart not scornful glances from those eyes
To wound thy lord, thy king, thy governor:
It blots thy beauty as frosts do bite the meads,*

Confounds thy fame as whirlwinds shake fair buds,
And in no sense is meet or amiable.
Thy husband is thy lord, thy life, thy keeper,
Thy head, thy sovereign; one that cares for thee,
And for thy maintenance commits his body
To painful labour both by sea and land,
To watch the night in storms, the day in cold,
Whilst thou liest warm at home, secure and safe;
And craves no other tribute at thy hands
But love, fair looks, and true obedience;
Too little payment for so great a debt.
Such duty as the subject owes the prince
Even such a woman oweth to her husband;
And when she is froward,* peevish, sullen, sour,
And not obedient to his honest will,
What is she but a foul contending rebel
And graceless traitor to her loving lord?
Why are our bodies soft and weak and smooth,
Unapt to toil and trouble in the world,
But that our soft conditions and our hearts
Should well agree with our external parts?
Come, come, you froward and unable worms!
My mind hath been as big as one of yours,
My heart as great, my reason haply more,
To bandy word for word and frown for frown;
But now I see our lances are but straws,
Our strength as weak, our weakness past compare,
That seeming to be most which we indeed least are.
Then vail your stomachs,* for it is no boot,*
And place your hands below your husband's foot:
In token of which duty, if he please,
My hand is ready; may it do him ease. 🙶

(*Act 5, scene 2, lines 136–79, with some cuts*)

GLOSSARY

meads – meadows
froward – wilful, difficult
vail your stomachs – abandon your obstinacy, swallow your pride
it is no boot – there's nothing else for it

All's Well That Ends Well

WHO ☞ *Helena, who, having recently been orphaned by the death of her father, has been taken into the care of the Countess.*

WHERE ☞ *A room in the Countess's house in Rossillion in southern France.*

WHO ELSE IS THERE ☞ *Helena is alone.*

WHAT IS HAPPENING ☞ *Though she should be crying out of grief for her dead father, Helena is instead shedding tears because of her hopeless love of Bertram, son of the Countess, who has adopted her. Bertram is about to leave the household.*

WHAT TO THINK ABOUT ☞

- *Helena knows she should be grieving for her father but can think only of Bertram.*
- *She feels she is not worthy of Bertram and expresses very low self-esteem.*
- *There is a strong mix of romance, love, sexual desire and even perhaps a death wish in the speech with Helena thinking of herself as a young deer wanting to be mated by a lion.*
- *Try to picture every detail of Bertram as Helena describes him. Add to the details as you work on the speech and think why Helena has chosen the ones she has.*

WHERE ELSE TO LOOK ☞ *In The Merchant of Venice both Jessica (p. 32) and Portia (p. 34) are caught between duty to their fathers and love for young men.*

Helena

" I think not on my father,
And these great tears grace his remembrance more
Than those I shed for him. What was he like?
I have forgot him. My imagination
Carries no favour in't but Bertram's.
I am undone! There is no living, none,
If Bertram be away. 'Twere all one
That I should love a bright particular star
And think to wed it, he is so above me.
In his bright radiance and collateral light
Must I be comforted, not in his sphere.
Th'ambition in my love thus plagues itself.
The hind* that would be mated by the lion
Must die for love. 'Twas pretty, though a plague,*
To see him every hour; to sit and draw
His archèd brows, his hawking eye, his curls,
In our heart's table* – heart too capable*
Of every line and trick of his sweet favour.
But now he's gone, and my idolatrous fancy
Must sanctify his relics.* **"**

(Act 1, scene 1, lines 78–97)

GLOSSARY

hind – deer
'Twas pretty, though a plague – it was enjoyable, albeit agonising
table – sketchpad
capable – receptive
sanctify his relics – worship the traces of his presence

All's Well That Ends Well

WHO ☞   *The Countess of Rossillion.*

WHERE ☞   *A room in the Countess's house in Rossillion in southern France.*

WHO ELSE IS THERE ☞   *Helena, who has been adopted by the Countess.*

WHAT IS HAPPENING ☞   *The Countess has taken the newly orphaned Helena under her protection. She wants to be a mother to Helena, but when she says this Helena does not welcome the news.*

WHAT TO THINK ABOUT ☞

- *The Countess is trying to find out why Helena will not accept her love.*
- *She gives Helena many opportunities to tell her the truth but Helena will not be honest with her.*
- *Allow time for the responses from Helena that – in this conflation of the scene – never come.*
- *Find the moment of revelation when the Countess realises that the problem is because Helena loves her son.*

WHERE ELSE TO LOOK ☞   *Just as the Countess is trying to get a response from her foster daughter, so Marina (Pericles, p. 60) is doing the same with the man who is her real father.*

Countess of Rossillion

❝ I am a mother to you. Nay, a mother,
Why not a mother? When I said 'a mother',
Methought you saw a serpent. What's in 'mother'
That you start at it? I say I am your mother,
And put you in the catalogue of those
That were enwombèd mine. 'Tis often seen
Adoption strives with nature, and choice breeds
A native slip to us from foreign seeds.*

You ne'er oppress'd me with a mother's groan,
Yet I express to you a mother's care –
God's mercy, maiden, does it curd* thy blood
To say I am thy mother? What's the matter,
That this distemper'd messenger of wet,
The many-colour'd Iris, rounds thine eye?*
Why? That you are my daughter?
I say I am your mother. What, pale again?
My fear hath catch'd your fondness! Now I see
The mystery of your loveliness, and find
Your salt tears' head.* Now to all sense 'tis gross:*
You love my son. Invention is asham'd
Against the proclamation of thy passion
To say thou dost not. Therefore tell me true,
But tell me then 'tis so, for look, thy cheeks
Confess it, t'one to th'other, and thine eyes
See it so grossly shown in thy behaviours
That in their kind they speak it. Only sin
And hellish obstinacy tie thy tongue,
That truth should be suspected. Speak, is't so?
If it be so, you have wound a goodly clew;*
If it be not, forswear't.* Howe'er, I charge thee,
As heaven shall work in me for thine avail,
To tell me truly. 99

(*Act 1, scene 3, lines 133–79*)

GLOSSARY

choice breeds / A native slip to us from foreign seeds – choosing to grow
   something from foreign seeds can make a native plant, i.e. it is
   possible to love an adopted child like a natural one
curd – congeal
*this distemper'd messenger of wet, / The many-colour'd Iris, rounds thine
   eye* – Helena is crying
head – source
gross – obvious
wound a goodly clew – (proverbial) made a nice ball of wool, i.e. made a
   proper meal of it
forswear't – deny it

Twelfth Night

WHO ☞   *Olivia, a countess in mourning for her brother.*

WHERE ☞   *A room in her house in Illyria, a semi-mythical place on the coast of present-day Croatia.*

WHO ELSE IS THERE ☞   *For the first part of the speech Olivia is alone. She calls in her servant Malvolio and, once he has left, is alone again.*

WHAT IS HAPPENING ☞   *Count Orsino has sent his servant Cesario (in fact the disguised Viola) as a go-between to Olivia with whom he is in love. After Cesario has left, Olivia remembers their conversation and realises that she is falling in love with him – catching 'the plague'. She calls to her servant Malvolio and sends him after 'the man' in the hope that he will return.*

WHAT TO THINK ABOUT ☞

- *Olivia is remembering her conversation with Cesario, picturing him as she describes him.*
- *She uses the formal 'your' followed by the more intimate 'thou'.*
- *She points out five things that make him special.*
- *Decide at what point she realises she is falling in love and how sudden or gradual that realisation is. Decide why she calls love 'the plague'.*
- *Decide at what point the thought of sending Malvolio after Cesario comes into her head.*
- *Decide what it is she fears and what she thinks of fate. She might be thrilled, frightened, excited, nervous, restless, confused, or a combination of all these things.*
- *She has to calm herself down with 'Soft, soft.'*

WHERE ELSE TO LOOK ☞   *Another woman realising she is in love as she recalls a recent conversation is Phoebe (As You Like It, p. 40).*

Olivia

❝ 'What is your parentage?'
'Above my fortunes, yet my state is well:
I am a gentleman.' I'll be sworn thou art.
Thy tongue, thy face, thy limbs, actions and spirit,
Do give thee five-fold blazon* – not too fast! Soft, soft.
Unless the master were the man. How now?
Even so quickly may one catch the plague?
Methinks I feel this youth's perfections
With an invisible and subtle stealth
To creep in at mine eyes. Well, let it be.
– What ho, Malvolio!
Run after that same peevish messenger,
The County's* man. He left this ring behind him,
Would I or not. Tell him I'll none of it.
Desire him not to flatter with his lord,
Nor hold him up with hopes; I am not for him.
If that the youth will come this way tomorrow,
I'll give him reasons for't. Hie thee, Malvolio –
I do I know not what, and fear to find
Mine eye too great a flatterer for my mind.
Fate, show thy force; ourselves we do not owe.
What is decreed must be, and be this so. **❞**

(Act 1, scene 5, lines 272–94)

GLOSSARY

give thee five-fold blazon – declare your coat-of-arms five times over
   (Cesario's tongue, face, limbs, actions and spirit; only a gentleman
   was allowed a coat of arms)
County's – County = Count (i.e. Orsino)

Twelfth Night

WHO ☞ *Viola, a young woman of noble birth, disguised as 'Cesario'.*

WHERE ☞ *A street in Illyria, a semi-mythical place on the coast of present-day Croatia, near the house of the countess Olivia.*

WHO ELSE IS THERE ☞ *Viola is alone.*

WHAT IS HAPPENING ☞ *Shipwrecked in Illyria, Viola has disguised herself as a boy, 'Cesario', become employed by the Duke Orsino, and fallen in love with him. Her master, not realising she is a girl, has sent her as a go-between to Olivia with whom he is in love. But Olivia has now fallen in love with 'Cesario' and sent her servant Malvolio after him with a ring pretending that Cesario left it behind.*

WHAT TO THINK ABOUT ☞

- *Viola could be talking just to herself or using the audience as a confidant.*

- *Viola is alone but dressed as Cesario. 'I am the man,' she says. Play with the possibilities of being both genders.*

- *Decide at what point it dawns on her that Olivia has fallen in love with her.*

- *Be clear in the storytelling both for Viola and the audience. Work through the love triangle as Viola explains who is in love with whom. Decide how Olivia's love affects Viola and how deeply Viola is in love with Orsino, her master.*

- *Decide whether Viola is enjoying the 'wickedness' of her disguise or whether it is a burden. Think about why she calls herself a 'monster'.*

WHERE ELSE TO LOOK ☞ *Rosalind's epilogue to the audience plays with the confusion of cross-dressing (As You Like It, p. 42). Imogen (Cymbeline, p. 120) is also dressed in male clothes.*

Viola

" I left no ring with her. What means this lady?
Fortune forbid my outside have not charm'd her!
She made good view of me, indeed so much
That sure methought her eyes had lost her tongue,
For she did speak in starts distractedly.
She loves me, sure: the cunning of her passion
Invites me in this churlish messenger.
None of my lord's ring? Why, he sent her none!
I am the man. If it be so, as 'tis,
Poor lady, she were better love a dream.
Disguise, I see thou art a wickedness,
Wherein the pregnant enemy* does much.
How easy is it for the proper false
In women's waxen hearts to set their forms!*
Alas, our frailty is the cause, not we,
For such as we are made of, such we be.
How will this fadge?* My master loves her dearly,
And I – poor monster – fond as much on him;
And she, mistaken, seems to dote on me.
What will become of this? As I am man,
My state is desperate for my master's love.
As I am woman – now alas the day –
What thriftless sighs shall poor Olivia breathe!
O time, thou must untangle this, not I:
It is too hard a knot for me t'untie! **"**

(Act 2, scene 2, lines 16–40)

GLOSSARY

pregnant enemy – resourceful Satan
for the proper false / In women's waxen hearts to set their forms – for
    actual men, as attractive as they are deceitful, to impress women's
    hearts, like a signet ring on sealing wax, and stamp their presence
    there
fadge – turn out

The Winter's Tale

WHO ☞ *Hermione, Queen of Sicilia, wife to King Leontes.*

WHERE ☞ *A court of justice in Sicilia.*

WHO ELSE IS THERE ☞ *King Leontes, Paulina (a Lady of the Court), Lords, Officers and Ladies.*

WHAT IS HAPPENING ☞ *Accused by her husband of adultery with Polixenes, Hermione defends herself to Leontes and the court.*

WHAT TO THINK ABOUT ☞

- *Hermione has been brought to court from prison where she has given birth to a baby daughter. She has only just heard the accusations made to her: that she has committed adultery and conspired to kill the King her husband.*

- *This is both a private and a public scene. Hermione defends herself to her husband, but in front of the court. Decide which lines are played to her husband and which to the court.*

- *She sees herself as daughter (of a great King), wife and mother. How are these roles played within the speech?*

- *Hermione must be exhausted. She has been in prison and has just given birth. Shortly after this speech she will faint and be taken away, apparently to die.*

WHERE ELSE TO LOOK ☞ *Hermione has a similar speech (see next page). Queen Katharine defends herself to Henry VIII (p. 84).*

Hermione

❝ Since what I am to say must be but that
Which contradicts my accusation, and
The testimony on my part no other
But what comes from myself, it shall scarce boot me
To say 'not guilty': mine integrity
Being counted falsehood, shall, as I express it,

Be so receiv'd. But thus, if powers divine
Behold our human actions (as they do),
I doubt not then but innocence shall make
False accusation blush, and tyranny
Tremble at patience.* You, my lord, best know,
Who least will seem to do so, my past life
Hath been as continent,* as chaste, as true,
As I am now unhappy; which is more
Than history can pattern, though devis'd
And play'd to take spectators.* For behold me,
A fellow of the royal bed, which owe
A moiety* of the throne, a great king's daughter,
The mother to a hopeful prince, here standing
To prate and talk for life, and honour, 'fore
Who please to come, and hear. For life, I prize it
As I weigh grief, which I would spare. For honour,
'Tis a derivative from me to mine,
And only that I stand for. I appeal
To your own conscience, sir, before Polixenes
Came to your court, how I was in your grace,
How merited to be so. Since he came,
With what encounter so uncurrent, I
Have strain'd to appear thus;* if one jot beyond
The bound of honour, or in act, or will
That way inclining, harden'd be the hearts
Of all that hear me, and my near'st of kin
Cry fie upon my grave. **99**

(*Act 3, scene 2, lines 21–53*)

GLOSSARY

patience – strength, fortitude, endurance
continent – virtuous, faithful
though devis'd / And play'd to take spectators – even if a play was made
of it
moiety – half, equal part
Polixenes – pronounced '*Po-licks-in-ease*'
*Since he came, / With what encounter so uncurrent, I / Have strain'd to
appear thus* – what has happened since Polixenes came to stay that
warrants my being brought to this court?

The Winter's Tale

WHO ☞ *Hermione, Queen of Sicilia, wife to King Leontes.*

WHERE ☞ *A court of justice in Sicilia.*

WHO ELSE IS THERE ☞ *King Leontes, Paulina (a Lady of the Court), Lords, Officers and Ladies.*

WHAT IS HAPPENING ☞ *Accused by her husband King Leontes of adultery and conspiring to have him murdered, Queen Hermione tells Leontes that his threats are useless and asks that the oracle of the god Apollo be her judge.*

WHAT TO THINK ABOUT ☞

- *Her husband Leontes is threatening her. Hermione uses just four short words to cut him short: 'Sir, spare your threats.'*
- *She tells of the terrible things that have happened to her: losing her husband's love, not being allowed to see her son (her second joy), having her new born daughter (her third joy) taken away from her. Do not let them become a list. Each is a different source of pain and suffering.*
- *She talks not just as a Queen but compares herself to all women.*
- *The speech is for the most part directed at the King but at the end she turns to everyone else in the room.*
- *She ends as she began with four short words.*

WHERE ELSE TO LOOK ☞ *Hermione has another such speech, for which see the previous page. Queen Katharine has to defend herself in court in front of her husband the King (Henry VIII, p. 84).*

Hermione

❝ Sir, spare your threats.
The bug* which you would fright me with I seek.
To me can life be no commodity;
The crown and comfort of my life, your favour,
I do give lost; for I do feel it gone,
But know not how it went. My second joy
And first fruits of my body, from his presence
I am barr'd, like one infectious. My third comfort,
Starr'd most unluckily,* is from my breast
(The innocent milk in its most innocent mouth)
Hal'd out to murder. Myself on every post
Proclaim'd a strumpet. With immodest hatred
The child-bed privilege denied, which longs*
To women of all fashion. Lastly, hurried
Here, to this place, i' th' open air, before
I have got strength of limit. Now, my liege,
Tell me what blessings I have here alive,
That I should fear to die? Therefore proceed.
But yet hear this. Mistake me not. No life,
I prize it not a straw, but for mine honour,
Which I would free – if I shall be condemn'd
Upon surmises (all proofs sleeping else,
But what your jealousies awake) I tell you
'Tis rigour* and not law. Your honours all,
I do refer me to the oracle:*
Apollo be my judge! **❞**

(Act 3, scene 2, lines 90–115)

GLOSSARY

bug – terror
Starr'd most unluckily – destined by the stars for an unlucky fate
longs – belongs
refer me to the oracle – Hermione asks that the mouth-piece of the god
    Apollo be asked to reveal the truth
rigour – severity

The Winter's Tale

WHO ☞ *Paulina, a Lady at the court of King Leontes of Sicilia.*

WHERE ☞ *A court of justice in Sicilia.*

WHO ELSE IS THERE ☞ *King Leontes, Lords, Officers and Ladies.*

WHAT IS HAPPENING ☞ *King Leontes has wrongly accused his wife Queen Hermione of adultery with Polixenes. Paulina comes into the court to bring the news of her death.*

WHAT TO THINK ABOUT ☞

- *Paulina has come to say that the Queen is dead, but before getting to this she publicly accuses the King of all his wrong doings that have led to this point.*
- *Paulina is being brave to say such things to the King. The punishments she is risking are real.*
- *Make each of these accusations individual: the betrayal of his friend King Polixenes; ordering his adviser Camillo to kill Polixenes; ordering his daughter murdered and left to be eaten by crows; the death of the young Prince.*
- *Decide what the lords that she turns to at the end of her speech might be thinking and feeling and how that could affect the way in which she makes her accusations.*
- *She might feel relieved, angry, exhausted and scared once she has said that the Queen is dead.*

WHERE ELSE TO LOOK ☞ *Women who stand up to men of power include Hermione (The Winter's Tale, pp. 54 and 56) and Lady Percy (Henry IV, Part Two, p. 70).*

Paulina

" What studied* torments, tyrant, hast for me?
What wheels? racks? fires? what flaying? boiling?
In leads or oils? what old or newer torture
Must I receive, whose every word deserves
To taste of thy most worst? Thy tyranny
(Together working with thy jealousies,
Fancies too weak for boys, too green and idle
For girls of nine) O, think what they have done,
And then run mad indeed. Stark mad. For all
Thy by-gone fooleries were but spices* of it.
That thou betray'dst Polixenes, 'twas nothing;
That did but show thee, of a fool, inconstant,
And damnable ingrateful. Nor was't much
Thou wouldst have poison'd good Camillo's honour,
To have him kill a king: poor trespasses,*
More monstrous standing by: whereof I reckon
The casting forth to crows thy baby-daughter
To be or none, or little though a devil
Would have shed water out of fire ere done't.
Nor is't directly laid to thee the death
Of the young prince, whose honourable thoughts
(Thoughts high for one so tender) cleft the heart
That could conceive a gross and foolish sire
Blemish'd his gracious dam.* This is not, no,
Laid to thy answer. But the last: O lords,
When I have said, cry 'woe!' The Queen, the Queen,
The sweet'st, dear'st creature's dead. And vengeance for't
Not dropp'd down yet. **"**

(Act 3, scene 2, lines 174–201)

GLOSSARY

studied – calculated
but spices – mere hints
poor trespasses – feeble sins
dam – wife

Pericles

WHO ☞ *Marina, daughter of Pericles, Prince of Tyre.*

WHERE ☞ *Aboard a boat off the coast of Mytilene (the present day Greek island of Lesbos).*

WHO ELSE IS THERE ☞ *Pericles. Helicanus (a Lord of Tyre), Lysimachus (Governor of Mytilene) and others are close by.*

WHAT IS HAPPENING ☞ *Pericles thinks his daughter Marina has died many years ago. Not knowing him to be her father, she comes to try to bring comfort to the grieving old man.*

WHAT TO THINK ABOUT ☞

- *Notice how Marina is keen to establish her status.*
- *Think what makes her decide to desist and whether she says this to herself or to the others waiting nearby.*
- *Decide what it is that glows upon her cheeks and whispers in her ear.*
- *Decide how she might react to the whispering voice.*
- *Marina tells the tragic tale of her life. Consider how she might feel about it.*

WHERE ELSE TO LOOK ☞ *Another daughter pleading with her father is Miranda (The Tempest, p. 20).*

Marina

" I am a maid,
My lord, that ne'er before invited eyes,
But have been gaz'd on like a comet. She speaks,
My lord, that maybe hath endur'd a grief
Might equal yours, if both were justly weigh'd.
Though wayward Fortune did malign my state,
My derivation was from ancestors
Who stood equivalent with mighty kings.
But time hath rooted out my parentage,
And to the world and awkward casualties
Bound me in servitude. I will desist,
But there is something glows upon my cheek,
And whispers in mine ear, 'Go not till he speak.'
The King my father did in Tarsus leave me;
Till cruel Cleon, with his wicked wife,
Did seek to murder me: and having woo'd
A villain to attempt it, who having drawn to do't,
A crew of pirates came and rescued me;
Brought me to Mytilene.* But, good sir,
Whither will you have me? Why do you weep?
It may be, you think me an impostor.
No, good faith,
I am the daughter to King Pericles,
If good King Pericles be. **"**

(*Act 5, scene 1, lines 85–97 and 172–81;*
two speeches conflated)

GLOSSARY

Mytilene – pronounced '*Mit-ee-lee-nee*'

The Histories

King John

WHO ☞ *Lady Constance, mother of Arthur, Duke of Brittany.*

WHERE ☞ *At Angers in France, c. 1200.*

WHO ELSE IS THERE ☞ *The Duke of Salisbury and Lady Constance's son Arthur.*

WHAT IS HAPPENING ☞ *The Duke of Salisbury brings news that France and England have made peace through the marriage of Lewis the Dauphin (oldest son of the King) of France and Blanche of Spain, niece of the English King John. Constance, mother of Arthur, Duke of Brittany, is angry at the new peace and curses the wedding that has thus deprived her son of succession to the English crown.*

WHAT TO THINK ABOUT ☞

- *Beware of playing the whole speech on one note of indignant, incredulous rage.*
- *Decide how much of Constance's anger is expressed directly at Salisbury and how much at each of the other characters she talks of.*
- *Decide why she uses the word 'fears' so many times and find different ways of delivering that word.*
- *Think how she might include her son in the scene.*
- *Decide why it is that Salisbury says nothing and whether Constance softens when she see the tears welling in his eyes.*

WHERE ELSE TO LOOK ☞ *Other women angry at those that have done them wrong include the Duchess of Gloucester and Queen Margaret (Henry VI, Part Two, pp. 76 and 78).*

Constance

" Gone to be married? Gone to swear a peace?
False blood to false blood join'd? Gone to be friends?
Shall Lewis have Blanche, and Blanche those provinces?
It is not so, thou hast misspoke, misheard,
Be well advis'd, tell o'er thy tale again.
It cannot be, thou dost but say 'tis so.
I trust I may not trust thee, for thy word
Is but the vain breath of a common man.
Believe me, I do not believe thee, man,
I have a King's oath to the contrary.
Thou shalt be punish'd for thus frighting me,
For I am sick, and capable of fears,
Oppress'd with wrongs and therefore full of fears,
A widow, husbandless, subject to fears,
A woman, naturally born to fears;
And though thou now confess thou didst but jest,
With my vex'd spirits, I cannot take a truce,
But they will quake and tremble all this day.
What dost thou mean by shaking of thy head?
Why dost thou look so sadly on my son?
What means that hand upon that breast of thine?
Why holds thine eye that lamentable rheum,*
Like a proud river peering o'er his bounds?
Be these sad signs confirmers of thy words?
Then speak again, not all thy former tale,
But this one word, whether thy tale be true. **"**

(*Act 3, scene 1, lines 1–26*)

GLOSSARY

lamentable rheum – sorrowful tears

Richard II

WHO ☞ *The Duchess of Gloucester.*

WHERE ☞ *A room in John of Gaunt's house in London, c. 1397.*

WHO ELSE IS THERE ☞ *John of Gaunt.*

WHAT IS HAPPENING ☞ *Thomas Mowbray, the Duke of Norfolk, has murdered the King's uncle, Thomas, Duke of Gloucester. The dead man's brother, John of Gaunt, and his wife, the Duchess of Gloucester, believe that he was murdered on the orders of King Richard. The Duchess pleads with Gloucester's brother, John of Gaunt, to avenge his death.*

WHAT TO THINK ABOUT ☞

- *The Duchess's love for her husband permeates all the speech. Note how she calls him 'Thomas, my dear lord, my life, my Gloucester', each of which can have a different tone and thought.*

- *The Duchess uses a number of different tactics with Gaunt in an attempt to get him to side with her. Find different tones for each of these tactics.*

- *It is a political speech demanding an outcome; it is also a speech about the bonds of family, and it is a speech that plays on Gaunt's self-interest.*

WHERE ELSE TO LOOK ☞ *Lady Percy (Henry IV, Part Two, p. 70) also cites the combination of family and politics in pleading her case.*

Duchess of Gloucester

❝ Finds brotherhood in thee no sharper spur?
Hath love in thy old blood no living fire?
Edward's seven sons,* whereof thyself art one,
Were as seven vials of his sacred blood,
Or seven fair branches springing from one root.
Some of those seven are dried by nature's course;
Some of those branches by the Destinies cut;
But Thomas, my dear lord, my life, my Gloucester,
One vial full of Edward's sacred blood,*
One flourishing branch of his most royal root,
Is crack'd, and all the precious liquor spilt,
Is hack'd down, and his summer leaves all faded,
By Envy's hand and Murder's bloody axe.
Ah, Gaunt, his blood was thine!* That bed, that womb,
That metal,* that self mould, that fashion'd thee,
Made him a man; and though thou liv'st and breath'st,
Yet art thou slain in him. Thou dost consent
In some large measure to thy father's death
In that thou seest thy wretched brother die,
Who was the model of thy father's life.
Call it not patience, Gaunt; it is despair.
In suffering thus thy brother to be slaughter'd,
Thou show'st the naked pathway to thy life,
Teaching stern Murder how to butcher thee.
That which in mean men we entitle patience
Is pale cold cowardice in noble breasts.
What shall I say? To safeguard thine own life,
The best way is to venge my Gloucester's death. **❞**

(Act 1, scene 2, lines 9–36)

GLOSSARY

Edward's seven sons – the seven sons of the previous King, Edward III,
    of whom the dead Gloucester and John of Gaunt are two
One vial full of Edward's sacred blood – as one of Edward's sons he
    contained Edward's blood
his blood was thine – as his brother his blood was yours
metal – substance

Henry IV, Part One

WHO ☞ *Lady Elizabeth 'Kate' Percy, wife of Henry 'Harry Hotspur' Percy.*

WHERE ☞ *Warkworth Castle, Northumberland, her home, c. 1403.*

WHO ELSE IS THERE ☞ *Her husband Harry Hotspur.*

WHAT IS HAPPENING ☞ *Harry Hotspur has just told his wife that he must leave her 'within these two hours'. Lady Percy questions her husband as to why he spends so much time on his own, demands he tell her his plans and explain why he talks of war in his sleep.*

WHAT TO THINK ABOUT ☞

- *Hotspur says nothing in response to his wife. This could be a factor in driving on her speech.*
- *We know from a later speech (see next page) how much Lady Percy loves and admires her husband.*
- *There is a feeling here of a woman who has lost the relationship she once had with her husband. Her words might be tinged with grief, sadness, anger, concern, love, desire, or a combination of any or all of these.*
- *Lady Percy has lost sleep as she has watched over her husband. Decide how this might affect the scene.*

WHERE ELSE TO LOOK ☞ *Portia (Julius Caesar, p. 102) is also distressed by her husband's nocturnal behaviour and demands to know his secrets.*

Lady Elizabeth Percy

❝ O my good lord, why are you thus alone?
For what offence have I this fortnight been
A banish'd woman from my Harry's bed?

Tell me, sweet lord, what is't that takes from thee
Thy stomach, pleasure and thy golden sleep?
Why dost thou bend thine eyes upon the earth,
And start so often when thou sit'st alone?
Why hast thou lost the fresh blood in thy cheeks;
And given my treasures and my rights of thee
To thick-ey'd musing and curs'd melancholy?*
In thy faint slumbers I by thee have watch'd,
And heard thee murmur tales of iron wars,
Speak terms of manage to thy bounding steed,
Cry 'Courage! To the field!' And thou hast talk'd
Of sallies and retires, of trenches, tents,
Of palisadoes,* frontiers, parapets,
Of basilisks,* of cannon, culverin,*
Of prisoners' ransom, and of soldiers slain,
And all the currents of a heady fight.
Thy spirit within thee hath been so at war,
And thus hath so bestirr'd thee in thy sleep,
That beads of sweat have stood upon thy brow
Like bubbles in a late-disturbèd stream,
And in thy face strange motions have appear'd,
Such as we see when men restrain their breath
On some great sudden hest.* O, what portents are these?
Some heavy business hath my lord in hand,
And I must know it, else he loves me not. **99**

(*Act 2, scene 3, lines 37–64*)

GLOSSARY

given my treasures and my rights of thee / To thick-ey'd musing and curs'd melancholy – ignored my love and my rights as a wife because of your depression
palisadoes – defences made of pointed stakes
basilisks – large cannons
culverin – small cannon
hest – command

Henry IV, Part Two

WHO ☞ *Lady Elizabeth 'Kate' Percy, wife of Henry 'Harry Hotspur' Percy.*

WHERE ☞ *Warkworth Castle, Northumberland, c. 1403.*

WHO ELSE IS THERE ☞ *The Earl of Northumberland (father of her recently killed husband) and his wife.*

WHAT IS HAPPENING ☞ *Her husband, Harry Hotspur, has been killed in battle by Harry Monmouth (later Henry V), Hotspur's calls to his father, the Earl of Northumberland, having gone unanswered. The Earl has now joined the rebel army. Lady Percy and his wife (her mother-in-law) try to dissuade him from going.*

WHAT TO THINK ABOUT ☞

- *Much of the speech paints a picture of her dead husband (referred to as Percy, Harry or Hotspur), bringing him to life.*
- *Imagine what Hotspur's 'thick' voice sounded like and how that might colour Lady Percy's speech as she recollects it.*
- *She may be lost in the past as she talks of her husband and her marriage and then return to the present when she accuses Northumberland of having abandoned him.*
- *Do not forget that Northumberland's wife is also present.*
- *Remember that Monmouth is the man who killed her husband.*

WHERE ELSE TO LOOK ☞ *Cleopatra (Antony and Cleopatra, pp. 116 and 118) speaks lovingly of the absent and later dead Antony.*

Lady Elizabeth Percy

❝ O yet, for God's sake, go not to these wars!
The time was, father, that you broke your word
When you were more endear'd to it than now;
When your own Percy, when my heart's dear Harry,
Threw many a northward look to see his father

Bring up his powers; but he did long in vain.
Who then persuaded you to stay at home?
There were two honours lost: yours and your son's.
For yours, the God of heaven brighten it!
For his, it stuck upon him as the sun
In the grey vault of heaven, and by his light
Did all the chivalry of England move
To do brave acts. He was indeed the glass*
Wherein the noble youth did dress themselves.
He had no legs that practis'd not his gait;
And speaking thick, which nature made his blemish,
Became the accents of the valiant;
For those that could speak low and tardily
Would turn their own perfection to abuse,
To seem like him. So that in speech, in gait,
In diet, in affections of delight,
In military rules, humours of blood,*
He was the mark and glass, copy and book,
That fashion'd others. And him – O wondrous him!
O miracle of men! – him did you leave,
Second to none, unseconded by you,
To look upon the hideous god of war
In disadvantage, to abide a field
Where nothing but the sound of Hotspur's name
Did seem defensible: so you left him.
Never, O never, do his ghost the wrong
To hold your honour more precise and nice
With others than with him! Let them alone.
The marshal and the archbishop are strong:
Had my sweet Harry had but half their numbers,
Today might I, hanging on Hotspur's neck,
Have talk'd of Monmouth's grave. **99**

(Act 2, scene 3 lines 9–45)

GLOSSARY

glass – looking-glass, mirror
humours of blood – there were four bodily fluids thought to govern a
    person's disposition: governance by the humour of blood would
    imply you were amorous, optimistic, passionate and courageous

Henry V

WHO ☞ *The Hostess of the Boar's Head Tavern, formerly Mistress Quickly.*

WHERE ☞ *Before a tavern in Eastcheap, London, c. 1414.*

WHO ELSE IS THERE ☞ *Her husband Pistol, their friends Nym, Bardolph and a boy.*

WHAT IS HAPPENING ☞ *The group are in mourning. Sir John Falstaff, a fat, lecherous old knight and their friend and leader has died. Bardolph has just asked whether his soul has gone to heaven or hell.*

WHAT TO THINK ABOUT ☞

- *The speech is a rich mixture of grief and humour. The Hostess is recounting the death of someone loved by the entire group.*
- *Picture the scene she is describing and fill in every detail as you talk about it.*
- *Imagine what Falstaff's voice was like as you recall his words.*
- *There is an accent of some kind in the Hostess's voice. Find one you are comfortable with and which works for the speech.*
- *Find the sadness in her feeling his cold feet and the humour as her hand moves further up her body.*

WHERE ELSE TO LOOK ☞ *The Nurse (Romeo and Juliet, p. 96) is another older comic character.*

The Hostess

❝ Nay, sure, he's not in hell. He's in Arthur's bosom,* if ever man went to Arthur's bosom. 'A made a finer end, and went away an it had been any christom* child. 'A parted e'en just between twelve and one, e'en at the turning o'th' tide. For after I saw him fumble with the sheets, and play with flowers, and smile upon his fingers' end, I knew there was but one way: for his nose was as sharp as a pen, and 'a babbled of green fields. 'How now, Sir John?' quoth I. 'What, man? Be o' good cheer!' So 'a cried out, 'God, God, God,' three or four times. Now I, to comfort him, bid him 'a should not think of God; I hoped there was no need to trouble himself with any such thoughts yet. So 'a bade me lay more clothes on his feet. I put my hand into the bed and felt them, and they were as cold as any stone. Then I felt to his knees, and so upward and upward, and all was as cold as any stone. **❞**

(Act 2, scene 3, line 9 onwards)

GLOSSARY

Arthur's bosom – a malapropism for Abraham's bosom, i.e. heaven
christom – christened

Henry VI, Part One

WHO ☞   *Joan la Pucelle (Joan of Arc), a shepherd girl.*

WHERE ☞   *The siege of Orléans, 1429.*

WHO ELSE IS THERE ☞   *Charles the Dauphin (oldest son of the King) of France and others.*

WHAT IS HAPPENING ☞   *Arriving amongst the besieged French troops at Orléans, the shepherd girl Joan of Arc explains how she had a vision of the mother of God and challenges the Dauphin to single combat to demonstrate her ability to join his forces.*

WHAT TO THINK ABOUT ☞

- *Joan starts this speech as 'a shepherd's daughter' and ends it as a 'warlike mate'. Find that extraordinary change as you work through her words.*

- *Her being visited by the Virgin Mary is a scene within the speech and can show us the childlike Joan and how the revelation transformed her.*

- *Decide how brave and daring she is being to present herself before the Dauphin in this way.*

- *Decide what it is about her presence and her way of speaking that convinces the Dauphin and the French troops to have her lead them.*

WHERE ELSE TO LOOK ☞   *Cross-dressing and the combination of gender roles within one speech can also be found with Viola (Twelfth Night, p. 52) and Rosalind (As You Like It, p. 42).*

Joan la Pucelle

❝ Dauphin, I am by birth a shepherd's daughter,
My wit untrain'd in any kind of art.
Heaven and Our Lady gracious hath it pleas'd
To shine on my contemptible estate.
Lo, whilst I waited on my tender lambs,
And to sun's parching heat display'd my cheeks,
God's mother deignèd to appear to me,
And in a vision full of majesty,
Will'd me to leave my base vocation,
And free my country from calamity.
Her aid she promis'd and assur'd success.
In complete glory she reveal'd herself.
And, whereas I was black and swart* before,
With those clear rays, which she infus'd* on me,
That beauty am I bless'd with which you may see.
Ask me what question thou canst possible,
And I will answer unpremeditated.
My courage try by combat, if thou dar'st,
And thou shalt find that I exceed my sex.
Resolve on this: thou shalt be fortunate,
If thou receive me for thy warlike mate. **❞**

(*Act 1, scene 2, lines 51–71*)

GLOSSARY

swart – swarthy
infus'd – shone, poured, distilled

Henry VI, Part Two

WHO ☞ *The Duchess of Gloucester.*

WHERE ☞ *A street in London, c. 1445.*

WHO ELSE IS THERE ☞ *Duke Humphrey of Gloucester and others.*

WHAT IS HAPPENING ☞ *Eleanor, Duchess of Gloucester, has been arrested for witchcraft and for conspiracy against the young King Henry. She has been publicly humiliated and enters with papers pinned to her accusing her of being a witch and 'in a white sheet, her feet bare, and a taper burning in her hand'. She is about to be exiled.*

WHAT TO THINK ABOUT ☞

- *Though the Duchess is talking to her husband, there are others looking on.*
- *For someone of such high status, to be led in public through the streets must be especially humiliating.*
- *The little word 'No' is a pivot in the middle of the speech.*
- *A focus of the Duchess's anger is Queen Margaret (the wife of the King who has conspired against her husband the Duke of Gloucester), whom she only refers to as 'her'.*
- *Though a speech of defeat, there are other emotions and forces to be found in it, such as anger, defiance, self-pity and confusion.*

WHERE ELSE TO LOOK ☞ *Hermione (The Winter's Tale, pp. 54 and 56) is another humiliated but publicly defiant woman.*

Duchess of Gloucester

66 Ah, Gloucester, teach me to forget myself.
For whilst I think I am thy married wife,
And thou a prince, Protector of this land,

Methinks I should not thus be led along,
Mail'd up in shame, with papers on my back,
And follow'd with a rabble, that rejoice
To see my tears, and hear my deep-fet* groans.
The ruthless flint doth cut my tender feet,
And when I start, the envious people laugh
And bid me be advisèd how I tread.
Ah, Humphrey, can I bear this shameful yoke?
Trow'st thou* that e'er I'll look upon the world,
Or count them happy that enjoy the sun?
No. Dark shall be my light, and night my day.
To think upon my pomp shall be my hell.
Sometime I'll say, 'I am Duke Humphrey's wife,
And he a prince, and ruler of the land.
Yet so he rul'd, and such a prince he was,
As he stood by, whilst I, his forlorn duchess,
Was made a wonder, and a pointing-stock*
To every idle rascal follower.'
But be thou mild, and blush not at my shame,
Nor stir at nothing, till the axe of death
Hang over thee, as sure it shortly will.
For Suffolk, he that can do all in all
With her, that hateth thee and hates us all,
And York, and impious Beaufort, that false priest,
Have all lim'd bushes to betray thy wings,*
And fly thou how thou canst, they'll tangle thee.
But fear not thou, until thy foot be snar'd,
Nor never seek prevention of thy foes. **"**

(Act 2, scene 4, lines 28–58)

GLOSSARY

deep-fet – from deep inside
trow'st thou – do you believe
pointing-stock – laughing stock
lim'd bushes to betray thy wings – bushes were covered in lime to trap
    birds

Henry VI, Part Two

WHO ☞ *Queen Margaret, wife of King Henry VI.*

WHERE ☞ *The Abbey of Bury St. Edmunds, where the Parliament are meeting, c. 1450.*

WHO ELSE IS THERE ☞ *King Henry, the Dukes of Buckingham, Suffolk and York, Cardinal Beaufort and the Earls of Salisbury and Warwick.*

WHAT IS HAPPENING ☞ *Before Parliament, King Henry's wife accuses Humphrey, Duke of Gloucester, the King's uncle, of planning a coup. It is him she is referring to throughout the speech.*

WHAT TO THINK ABOUT ☞

- *This is at the beginning of the scene and the King is wondering why Humphrey is not there.*
- *This is a highly political speech from a woman dominating a room full of the most powerful men in the country.*
- *Decide how the Queen deals with her gender in winning the men to her viewpoint.*

WHERE ELSE TO LOOK ☞ *Forceful speeches by Queens and other women of high rank include Hermione (The Winter's Tale, pp. 54 and 56) and Lady Percy (Henry IV, Part Two, p. 70).*

Queen Margaret

❝ Can you not see? Or will ye not observe
The strangeness of his alter'd countenance?
We know the time since he was mild and affable,
And if we did but glance a far-off look,
Immediately he was upon his knee,
That all the court admir'd him for submission:

But meet him now, and be it in the morn,
When everyone will give the time of day,
He knits his brow, and shows an angry eye,
And passeth by with stiff unbowèd knee,
Disdaining duty that to us belongs.
Small curs are not regarded when they grin,*
But great men tremble when the lion roars,
And Humphrey is no little man in England.
First note that he is near you in descent,
And should you fall, he as the next will mount.
Me seemeth then, it is no policy,
Respecting what a rancorous mind he bears,
And his advantage following your decease,
That he should come about your royal person,
Or be admitted to your highness' council.
By flattery hath he won the commons' * hearts.
And when he please to make commotion,
'Tis to be fear'd they all will follow him.
Now 'tis the spring, and weeds are shallow-rooted;
Suffer them now, and they'll o'ergrow the garden,
And choke the herbs for want of husbandry.
The reverent care I bear unto my lord
Made me collect these dangers in the duke.
If it be fond, call it a woman's fear;
Which fear, if better reasons can supplant,
I will subscribe, and say I wrong'd the duke. **

(*Act 3, scene 1, lines 4–35*)

GLOSSARY

grin – snarl
commons' - the common people's

Henry VI, Part Three

WHO ☞ *Queen Margaret, wife of King Henry VI.*

WHERE ☞ *The Parliament House, London, c. 1460.*

WHO ELSE IS THERE ☞ *Her husband the King, and Prince Edward their son.*

WHAT IS HAPPENING ☞ *King Henry's wife rails at him for disinheriting their son Edward by naming the Duke of York as his heir. She will raise an army against him by recruiting disaffected 'northern lords'.*

WHAT TO THINK ABOUT ☞

- *The first line might be to herself.*
- *Margaret is full of action and stronger at doing a man's work than her husband is. Think of the importance of gender in the speech.*
- *Her concerns are with family, power and politics. Plot those different concerns through the speech.*
- *When she talks of other characters have a picture of each of them in your mind.*
- *The Queen says she will not sleep with Henry until his decision is repealed. Decide what their sexual relationship might be like and how strong a threat that might be.*

WHERE ELSE TO LOOK ☞ *Lady Macbeth (Macbeth, p. 104) is another woman prepared to do a man's work.*

Queen Margaret

❝ Who can be patient in such extremes?
Ah, wretched man, would I had died a maid
And never seen thee, never borne thee son,
Seeing thou hast prov'd so unnatural a father.
Hath he deserv'd to lose his birthright thus?

Hadst thou but lov'd him half so well as I,
Or felt that pain which I did for him once,
Or nourish'd him as I did with my blood,
Thou wouldst have left thy dearest heart-blood there,
Rather than have that savage duke thine heir,
And disinherited thine only son.
Ah, timorous wretch,
Thou hast undone thyself, thy son, and me,
And giv'n unto the house of York such head,
As thou shalt reign but by their sufferance.
To entail him and his heirs unto the crown,
What is it, but to make thy sepulchre,*
And creep into it far before thy time?
Warwick is Chancellor and the Lord of Calais,
Stern Falconbridge commands the narrow seas,
The Duke is made Protector of the realm,
And yet shalt thou be safe? Such safety finds
The trembling lamb, environèd with wolves.
Had I been there, which am a silly woman,
The soldiers should have toss'd me on their pikes
Before I would have granted to that act.
But thou preferr'st thy life before thine honour.
And seeing thou dost, I here divorce myself,
Both from thy table, Henry, and thy bed,
Until that Act of Parliament be repeal'd
Whereby my son is disinherited.
The northern lords, that have forsworn thy colours,*
Will follow mine, if once they see them spread.
And spread they shall be, to thy foul disgrace,
And utter ruin of the house of York. 〞

(*Act 1, scene 1, lines 216–55, with some cuts*)

GLOSSARY

sepulchre – grave
forsworn thy colours – renounced your flags of battle (i.e. refused to
    fight for you)

Richard III

WHO ☞ *Lady Anne, newly married to King Richard III.*

WHERE ☞ *The Court, gathered at the Tower of London, c. 1485.*

WHO ELSE IS THERE ☞ *Queen Elizabeth, the old Duchess of York, Clarence's daughter and others.*

WHAT IS HAPPENING ☞ *Lady Anne explains to Queen Elizabeth and the Duchess of York how she came to fall in love with and marry the man who killed both her first husband and her father-in-law, King Henry VI.*

WHAT TO THINK ABOUT ☞

- *The curse Lady Anne put on the man who has become her husband earlier in the play has come true and she has been its victim.*
- *The scene is unusual in being made up almost entirely of women.*
- *She looks back on the 'honey words' with which Richard trapped her into this marriage and talks of how different her life is with him now.*
- *She looks to the inevitable future when he will 'be rid' of her.*
- *Decide what she wants as she explains to the other women the mistakes she has made and whether she is seeking understanding or forgiveness, or maybe just someone to listen to her.*

WHERE ELSE TO LOOK ☞ *Emilia (Othello, p. 114) has regrets about her marriage.*

Lady Anne

" When he that is my husband now
Came to me, as I follow'd Henry's corpse,
When scarce the blood was well wash'd from his hands
Which issued from my other angel husband,
And that dead saint which then I weeping follow'd –
O, when, I say, I look'd on Richard's face,
This was my wish: 'Be thou,' quoth I, 'accurs'd
For making me, so young, so old a widow;
And, when thou wed'st, let sorrow haunt thy bed,
And be thy wife – if any be so mad –
As miserable by the life of thee
As thou hast made me by my dear lord's death.'
Lo, ere I can repeat this curse again,
Within so small a time, my woman's heart
Grossly grew captive to his honey words,
And prov'd the subject of my own soul's curse,
Which ever since hath kept my eyes from rest;
For never yet one hour in his bed
Did I enjoy the golden dew of sleep
But with his timorous dreams was still awak'd.
Besides, he hates me for my father Warwick,
And will, no doubt, shortly be rid of me. **"**

(Act 4, scene 1, lines 65-87)

Henry VIII

WHO ☞ *Katharine of Aragon, Queen and first wife to King Henry VIII.*

WHERE ☞ *A hall in Blackfriars, London, where the court is assembled, June 1529.*

WHO ELSE IS THERE ☞ *Her husband King Henry VIII, the Archbishop of Canterbury, the bishops of Lincoln, Ely, Rochester and St Asalph, Cardinal Wolsey and Cardinal Campeius and many others.*

WHAT IS HAPPENING ☞ *Having failed to persuade the Pope to annul his marriage, King Henry has asked the Archbishop of Canterbury to grant him a divorce. At proceedings in the court, Queen Katharine, from Aragon in Spain and therefore 'a stranger', pleads with the King not to reject her after twenty years of marriage.*

WHAT TO THINK ABOUT ☞

- *This is both a personal and a public speech.*
- *It is a grand and formal scene with Katharine appearing before all the important figures of church and state.*
- *She is also appearing before the man who is both her husband and the King.*
- *Decide how Katharine copes with talking about the intimacies of her marriage in such a setting.*
- *Katharine talks of the twenty years of her marriage. Bring those years to mind during the speech.*
- *Katharine had six children of which only Mary survived. She has not borne the King a son and heir. All that child-bearing has had an effect on her and she might she feel she has failed as a wife and queen.*
- *Katharine will feel lonely as a foreigner in the English court.*

WHERE ELSE TO LOOK ☞ *Hermione (The Winter's Tale*
pp. 54 and 56) is another queen defending herself to her husband
in a public court.

Queen Katharine

❝ Sir, I desire you do me right and justice,
And to bestow your pity on me; for
I am a most poor woman, and a stranger,
Born out of your dominions; having here
No judge indifferent, nor no more assurance
Of equal friendship and proceeding. Alas, sir,
In what have I offended you? What cause
Hath my behaviour given to your displeasure,
That thus you should proceed to put me off,
And take your good grace from me? Heaven witness,
I have been to you a true and humble wife,
At all times to your will conformable;
Ever in fear to kindle your dislike,
Yea, subject to your countenance, glad or sorry
As I saw it inclin'd. When was the hour
I ever contradicted your desire?
Or made it not mine too?
Sir, call to mind,
That I have been your wife, in this obedience,
Upward of twenty years, and have been bless'd
With many children by you. If in the course
And process of this time, you can report,
And prove it too, against mine honour aught,
My bond to wedlock, or my love and duty,
Against your sacred person, in God's name,
Turn me away; and let the foul'st contempt
Shut door upon me, and so give me up
To the sharp'st kind of justice. **❞**

(Act 2, scene 4, lines 11–55, with some cuts)

The Tragedies

Troilus and Cressida

WHO ☞ *Cressida, a young Trojan woman.*

WHERE ☞ *Troy, the orchard of Cressida's uncle Pandarus, during the war between the ancient Greeks and the Trojans.*

WHO ELSE IS THERE ☞ *Troilus, with whom she is in love, and Pandarus, Cressida's uncle.*

WHAT IS HAPPENING ☞ *Troilus and Cressida have been brought together by Cressida's uncle Pandarus. Troilus asks Cressida why her love was so hard to win. Cressida confesses that her love only 'seemed' hard to win. She tells him that she loved him at first sight and ends by asking him to stop her mouth with a kiss.*

WHAT TO THINK ABOUT ☞

- *Cressida describes the early part of her own speech by saying that she has 'blabb'd'.*

- *Decide why Troilus says nothing.*

- *Notice how broken up with punctuation the speech is, with Cressida constantly interrupting herself.*

- *This is a very intimate scene but Cressida does not seem to mind if her uncle overhears.*

- *Picture this Troilus that she is talking to: what he looks like and what she loves about him.*

- *Decide whether there are moments that are to herself and not directed to him.*

- *Decide how much she wants him to stop her mouth with a kiss.*

WHERE ELSE TO LOOK ☞ *Also head over heels in love are Juliet (Romeo and Juliet, pp. 98 and 100), Portia (The Merchant of Venice, p. 34) and Helena (All's Well That Ends Well, p. 46).*

Cressida

66 Hard to seem won: but I was won, my lord,
With the first glance that ever – pardon me;
If I confess much, you will play the tyrant.
I love you now, but not till now so much
But I might master it; in faith, I lie.
My thoughts were like unbridled children grown
Too headstrong for their mother. See, we fools,
Why have I blabb'd? Who shall be true to us
When we are so unsecret to ourselves?
But though I lov'd you well, I woo'd you not,
And yet, good faith, I wish'd myself a man;
Or that we women had men's privilege
Of speaking first. Sweet, bid me hold my tongue,
For in this rapture I shall surely speak
The thing I shall repent. See, see, your silence,
Cunning in dumbness, from my weakness draws
My soul of counsel* from me. Stop my mouth. 99

(*Act 3, scene 2, lines 125–41*)

GLOSSARY

counsel – judgement, good sense (Troilus's silence is taking away all
    Cressida's good sense)

Coriolanus

WHO ☞ *Volumnia, mother to the valiant warrior Coriolanus.*

WHERE ☞ *Coriolanus's tent outside Rome, c. 400 BC.*

WHO ELSE IS THERE ☞ *Her son Coriolanus with his partner-in-arms Aufidius and their soldiers, Coriolanus's wife Virgilia, and his son Martius.*

WHAT IS HAPPENING ☞ *Coriolanus has joined the Volsces and is marching against his own Roman people. As Volumnia is pleading with Coriolanus to make peace, he turns away from her and she disowns him.*

WHAT TO THINK ABOUT ☞

- *Volumnia has a big audience that includes an army as well as her immediate family.*

- *It is also an intimate scene between mother and son.*

- *She tries a number of different approaches to her son in order to get her way; track these in the speech.*

- *Decide what she feels when Coriolanus turns from her.*

- *This is a woman who has probably never knelt before anyone until now and so kneeling might be emotionally and physically very difficult.*

WHERE ELSE TO LOOK ☞ *Other women angered at the political actions of close relatives include Lady Percy (Henry IV, Part Two, p. 70) and the Duchess of Gloucester (Henry VI, Part Two, p. 76).*

Volumnia

66 Thou know'st, great son,
The end of war's uncertain. But this certain,
That, if thou conquer Rome, the benefit
Which thou shalt thereby reap is such a name
Whose repetition will be dogg'd with curses;
Whose chronicle thus writ: 'The man was noble,
But with his last attempt, he wiped it out,
Destroy'd his country, and his name remains
To the ensuing age, abhorr'd.' Speak to me, son.
Think'st thou it honourable for a noble man
Still to remember wrongs? Daughter, speak you.
He cares not for your weeping. Speak thou, boy,
Perhaps thy childishness will move him more
Than can our reasons. There's no man in the world
More bound to 's mother, yet here he lets me prate
Like one i'th' stocks. Thou hast never in thy life
Show'd thy dear mother any courtesy.
He turns away:
Down, ladies. Let us shame him with our knees.
To his surname Coriolanus 'longs more pride
Than pity to our prayers. Down. An end,
This is the last. So, we will home to Rome,
And die among our neighbours. Nay, behold us,
This boy, that cannot tell what he would have,
But kneels, and holds up hands for fellowship,
Does reason our petition with more strength
Than thou hast to deny't. Come, let us go.
This fellow had a Volscian to his mother.
His wife is in Corioles, and his child
Like him by chance. Yet give us our dispatch.
I am hush'd until our city be a-fire,
And then I'll speak a little. **99**

(Act 5, scene 3, lines 138–83, with some cuts)

Titus Andronicus

WHO ☞ *Tamora, Queen of the Goths.*

WHERE ☞ *In ancient Rome.*

WHO ELSE IS THERE ☞ *Titus Andronicus with his sons and the Tribunes and Senators of Rome, two of Tamora's sons, Aaron the Moor and 'others as many as can be.'*

WHAT IS HAPPENING ☞ *The defeated Queen of the Goths pleads with Titus for the life of her eldest son, whom he has just ordered to be killed.*

WHAT TO THINK ABOUT ☞

- *This is a big scene as the stage direction from the First Folio indicates, calling for 'as many as can be' on stage.*
- *Tamora has a short public moment to save herself and her son.*
- *She has to hold and quieten the crowd with her opening three words; she then has to get Titus's attention by flattery and conceding defeat; and then she has to plead as a mother. All of this is in just three lines.*
- *Think of her audience and how big a public speech it might be.*
- *Decide how she sees the effect of her words as she speaks and when and why she thinks to compare Titus to a god.*

WHERE ELSE TO LOOK ☞ *Hermione (The Winter's Tale, pp. 54 and 56) also publicly fights for life.*

Tamora

“ Stay, Roman brethren, gracious conqueror,
Victorious Titus, rue the tears I shed,
A mother's tears in passion for her son.
And if thy sons were ever dear to thee,
O, think my son to be as dear to me.
Sufficeth not* that we are brought to Rome
To beautify thy triumphs and return
Captive to thee, and to thy Roman yoke,
But must my sons be slaughter'd in the streets,
For valiant doings in their country's cause?
O! If to fight for king and commonweal
Were piety in thine, it is in these.
Andronicus, stain not thy tomb with blood.
Wilt thou draw near the nature of the gods?
Draw near them then in being merciful,
Sweet mercy is nobility's true badge,
Thrice noble Titus, spare my first-born son. ”

(*Act 1, scene 1, lines 104–20*)

GLOSSARY

Sufficeth not – is it not enough

Titus Andronicus

WHO ☞ *Tamora, Queen of the Goths.*

WHERE ☞ *A remote part of the forest outside Rome, in ancient times.*

WHO ELSE IS THERE ☞ *Aaron, her secret lover.*

WHAT IS HAPPENING ☞ *Tamora, the scheming Queen of the Goths, has just been married to the Roman Emperor Saturninus. She has a lover in the court, Aaron the Moor. Here she is alone with her lover in a remote spot outside the city walls.*

WHAT TO THINK ABOUT ☞

- *This is a secret affair in a lonely place. Decide how Tamora might express that in the way she delivers her speech.*

- *Decide how much time the lovers have and what the chances are of their being caught.*

- *Decide how much Tamora is in love with Aaron, how much she lusts after him and what it is about him that she finds attractive.*

- *Play with being seductive in her words, demeanour and actions.*

- *Think what it says about Tamora's character that it is traditionally the male lover who invites his female beloved to sit and canoodle with him by a country stream.*

WHERE ELSE TO LOOK ☞ *Erotic desire can also be found with Juliet (Romeo and Juliet, p. 100) and Cleopatra (Antony and Cleopatra, p. 116).*

Tamora

❝ My lovely Aaron, wherefore look'st thou sad,
When everything doth make a gleeful boast?
The birds chant melody on every bush,
The snake lies rollèd in the cheerful sun,
The green leaves quiver with the cooling wind,
And make a chequer'd shadow on the ground.
Under their sweet shade, Aaron, let us sit,
And, whilst the babbling echo mocks the hounds,
Replying shrilly to the well-tun'd horns,
As if a double hunt were heard at once,
Let us sit down, and mark their yelping noise.
And, after conflict such as was supposed
The wandering prince and Dido* once enjoy'd,
When with a happy storm they were surprised
And curtain'd with a counsel-keeping cave,
We may, each wreathèd in the other's arms,
Our pastimes* done, possess a golden slumber,
Whiles hounds and horns, and sweet melodious birds
Be unto us, as is a nurse's song
Of lullaby, to bring her babe asleep. **❞**

(*Act 2, scene 3, lines 10–29*)

GLOSSARY

wandering prince and Dido – the shipwrecked Aeneas and the Queen of
    Carthage
pastimes – sexual pleasures

Romeo and Juliet

WHO ☞   *The Nurse who has looked after Juliet since the day she was born.*

WHERE ☞   *The Capulet's house in Verona.*

WHO ELSE IS THERE ☞   *Lady Capulet, Juliet's mother.*

WHAT IS HAPPENING ☞   *When Lady Capulet mentions Juliet's age, the Nurse remembers the day she was born even better than her own mother does.*

WHAT TO THINK ABOUT ☞

- *There are possibilities for a wide range of emotions in this speech including love, nostalgia, remembered grief, happiness and sadness.*
- *The Nurse has happy memories of bringing up Juliet but talking about them brings up other memories of her own daughter Susan and of her husband, both of whom are now dead.*
- *She is remembering harvest time. Think of the details of high summer that will infuse her memories.*
- *Picture her husband and the sound of his voice as she talks about him.*

WHERE ELSE TO LOOK ☞   *Lady Percy (Henry IV, Part Two, p. 70) remembers a dead husband in a very different situation.*

Nurse

❝ Even or odd, of all days in the year
Come Lammas Eve* at night shall she be fourteen.
Susan and she, God rest all Christian souls,
Were of an age. Well, Susan is with God,
She was too good for me. But, as I said,
On Lammas Eve at night shall she be fourteen,
That shall she, marry,* I remember it well.
'Tis since the earthquake now eleven years,

he was wean'd, I never shall forget it,
the days of the year, upon that day.
For I had then laid wormwood to my dug,*
Sitting in the sun under the dove-house wall;
My lord and you were then at Mantua.
Nay, I do bear a brain. But as I said,
When it did taste the wormwood on the nipple
Of my dug and felt it bitter, pretty fool,
To see it tetchy and fall out with the dug!
'Shake!' quoth the dove-house,* 'twas no need, I trow,
To bid me trudge.*
And since that time it is eleven years,
For then she could stand alone, nay by the rood
She could have run, and waddled all about.
For even the day before she broke her brow,
And then my husband, God be with his soul,
'A was a merry man, took up the child.
'Yea,' quoth he, 'dost thou fall upon thy face?
Thou wilt fall backward when thou hast more wit,
Wilt thou not, Jule?' and, by my holy-dam,
The pretty wretch left crying, and said 'Ay.'
To see now how a jest shall come about!
I warrant, an I should live a thousand years,
I never should forget it. 'Wilt thou not, Jule?' quoth he,
And, pretty fool, it stinted* and said 'Ay.' 🙿

(*Act 1, scene 3, lines 18–50*)

GLOSSARY

Lammas Eve – 31 July, the day before Harvest Festival
marry – certainly
laid wormwood to my dug – put a bitter-tasting plant on her breast (to
  wean the child)
'Shake!' quoth the dove-house – all the doves in the dove-house told
  her to shake a leg, i.e. hurry up
trudge – leave
stinted – stopped

Romeo and Juliet

WHO ☞ *Juliet, daughter of the wealthy Capulet family.*

WHERE ☞ *Her room in the Capulets' house in Verona.*

WHO ELSE IS THERE ☞ *Juliet is alone.*

WHAT IS HAPPENING ☞ *Juliet is waiting for her nurse to bring news from Romeo, with whom she has just fallen in love.*

WHAT TO THINK ABOUT ☞

- *Juliet has only just fallen in love.*
- *She is desperate for some news from Romeo and impatiently tries to find reasons for the nurse's delay.*
- *Though there is urgency in her words, Juliet has time to fill and nothing else to do except talk to herself, so the speech need not be hurried.*
- *Find ways of physically showing Juliet's restlessness.*
- *Now in love herself, she understands for the first time why images of love are portrayed the way they are.*
- *Her youth is emphasised by her attitude to older people.*
- *Her train of thought is interrupted by the arrival of the nurse and her servant.*

WHERE ELSE TO LOOK ☞ *Also head over heels in love are Helena (*All's Well That Ends Well, *p. 46) and Cressida (*Troilus and Cressida, *p. 88).*

Juliet

" The clock struck nine when I did send the nurse,
In half an hour she promis'd to return,
Perchance she cannot meet him. That's not so.
O, she is lame, love's heralds should be thoughts,
Which ten times faster glides than the sun's beams,
Driving back shadows over louring* hills.
Therefore do nimble-pinion'd* doves draw love,
And therefore hath the wind-swift Cupid wings.
Now is the sun upon the highmost hill
Of this day's journey, and from nine till twelve
Is three long hours, yet she is not come.
Had she affections and warm youthful blood,
She would be as swift in motion as a ball,
My words would bandy* her to my sweet love,
And his to me,
But old folks, many feign as they were dead,
Unwieldy, slow, heavy, and pale as lead.
O God, she comes, O honey nurse, what news?
Hast thou met wit him? Send thy man away. **"**

(*Act 2, scene 4, lines 1–19*)

GLOSSARY

louring – gloomy
nimble-pinion'd – swift-winged
bandy – join, hurry

Romeo and Juliet

WHO ☞   *Juliet, daughter of the wealthy Capulet family.*

WHERE ☞   *Her room in the Capulets' house in Verona.*

WHO ELSE IS THERE ☞   *Juliet is alone.*

WHAT IS HAPPENING ☞   *The newly married Juliet waits for her husband Romeo, not realising that he has just killed her cousin Tybalt and been banished by the Duke.*

WHAT TO THINK ABOUT ☞

- *Juliet is desperate for night to come so she can be with Romeo.*

- *Her speech is full of elaborate romantic imagery. Decide how much of this she is making up as she speaks it and where it comes from.*

- *It is a very sensual speech. Picture what the Romeo she is thinking of looks, sounds, tastes, smells and feels like. Work your way through the speech with all your senses.*

- *It is also a very erotic speech. She has married Romeo but not yet spent the night with him – he has 'not yet enjoy'd' her.*

- *The word 'die' can also mean to orgasm and could indicate the degree of sexual desire in the speech.*

- *Juliet describes herself as being like 'an impatient child'. Decide how this might show itself in her speech and movements.*

WHERE ELSE TO LOOK ☞   *Cleopatra (Antony and Cleopatra, p. 116) also talks erotically about her absent lover.*

Juliet

❝ Gallop apace, you fiery-footed steeds,
Towards Phoebus'* lodging, such a wagoner
As Phaeton* would whip you to the west,
And bring in cloudy night immediately.
Spread thy close curtain, love-performing night,
That runaway's eyes may wink, and Romeo

Leap to these arms, untalk'd of and unseen.
Lovers can see to do their amorous rites,
By their own beauties. Or if love be blind,
It best agrees with night. Come, civil night,
Thou sober-suited matron all in black,
And learn me how to lose a winning match,
Play'd for a pair of stainless maidenhoods.
Hood my unmann'd blood bating in my cheeks*
With thy black mantle, till strange love grow bold,
Think true love acted simple modesty.
Come night, come Romeo, come thou day in night;
For thou wilt lie upon the wings of night
Whiter than new snow upon a raven's back.
Come gentle night, come loving, black-brow'd night.
Give me my Romeo, and when I shall die,
Take him and cut him out in little stars,
And he will make the face of heaven so fine,
That all the world will be in love with night,
And pay no worship to the garish sun.
O, I have bought the mansion of a love,
But not possess'd it, and, though I am sold,
Not yet enjoy'd. So tedious is this day
As is the night before some festival
To an impatient child that hath new robes
And may not wear them. O, here comes my nurse.

   Enter Nurse.

And she brings news; and every tongue that speaks
But Romeo's name, speaks heavenly eloquence.
Now, nurse, what news? **99**

(*Act 3, scene 2, lines 1–34*)

GLOSSARY

Phoebus – Roman god of the sun (pronounced '*Fee-bus*')
Phaeton – Greek god of the sun (pronounced '*Fie-yet-on*')
Hood my unmann'd blood bating in my cheeks – cover my uncontrollable
   blood beating in my cheeks, i.e. making her face red

Julius Caesar

WHO ☞ *Portia, wife of Brutus, who is plotting to kill Julius Caesar.*

WHERE ☞ *The garden of her house in Rome, c. 44 BC.*

WHO ELSE IS THERE ☞ *Brutus, her husband. The young servant Lucius is asleep nearby.*

WHAT IS HAPPENING ☞ *Once again, her husband Brutus has crept from their bed and left her alone. Portia finds him and pleads with him to tell her the cause of his strange behaviour.*

WHAT TO THINK ABOUT ☞

- *It is the early hours of the morning. Use that to create a sense of time and atmosphere.*
- *There is an air of conspiracy. Portia will not want to wake anyone, and there is a young servant asleep close by.*
- *Consider how often and how long Portia has been lying awake and what makes her unable to bear her anxieties any longer.*
- *Decide what might have been going through Portia's mind as she wondered what her husband was being so secret about.*
- *Think about the history of their marriage and why this conversation is so difficult for them both.*
- *Portia thinks it is unhealthy to be out at night. She is as keen for both to go inside as she is to find out her husband's secrets.*

WHERE ELSE TO LOOK ☞ *Lady Percy (Henry IV, Part One, p. 68) also pleads with her husband to tell her what is on his mind.*

Portia

❝ Y'ave ungently, Brutus,
Stole from my bed; and yesternight at supper
You suddenly arose and walk'd about,
Musing and sighing, with your arms across,
And when I ask'd you what the matter was,
You star'd upon me with ungentle looks.

I urg'd you further; then you scratch'd your head,
And too impatiently stamp'd with your foot.
Yet I insisted; yet you answer'd not,
But, with an angry wafture of your hand,
Gave sign for me to leave you. So I did,
Fearing to strengthen that impatience
Which seem'd too much enkindled, and withal
Hoping it was but an effect of humour,
Which sometime hath his hour with every man.
It will not let you eat, nor talk, nor sleep,
And could it work so much upon your shape
As it hath much prevail'd on your condition,
I should not know you, Brutus. Dear my lord,
Make me acquainted with your cause of grief.
Is Brutus sick? And is it physical
To walk unbracèd* and suck up the humours
Of the dank morning? What, is Brutus sick?
And will he steal out of his wholesome bed,
To dare the vile contagion of the night
And tempt the rheumy and unpurgèd* air
To add unto his sickness? No, my Brutus,
You have some sick offence within your mind,
Which by the right and virtue of my place
I ought to know of. And upon my knees
I charm you by my once commended beauty,
By all your vows of love, and that great vow
Which did incorporate and make us one,
That you unfold to me – your self, your half –
Why you are heavy, and what men tonight
Have had to resort to you, for here have been
Some six or seven who did hide their faces
Even from darkness. **"**

(Act 2, scene 1, lines 236–77, with some cuts)

GLOSSARY

physical . . . unbracèd – therapeutic . . . without protection
rheumy and unpurgèd – damp and unpurified

Macbeth

WHO ☞ *Lady Macbeth, wife of Macbeth, a general in King Duncan's army.*

WHERE ☞ *A room in Macbeth's castle at Inverness, historically the mid-11th century.*

WHO ELSE IS THERE ☞ *Lady Macbeth is alone.*

WHAT IS HAPPENING ☞ *Lady Macbeth has just read a letter from her husband who is away at war. In it he has told of meeting three witches who have prophesied that he will become King. She is interrupted by news that the present King, Duncan, is on his way to her castle. Lady Macbeth calls on spirits to help her kill him and so help her husband attain the crown.*

WHAT TO THINK ABOUT ☞

- *Lady Macbeth talks of 'my' battlements. That one possessive word indicates her character and the situation.*

- *Decide why she needs to call on spirits, whether she has done this before and how scary a thing this might be to do. There is the sense of an invocation, of a magic spell, in her words. Decide at what point she imagines the spirits arrive. Allow time for them to appear to her.*

- *Lady Macbeth wishes she could do the things a man can do. Decide what she feels about her body and how might this be expressed physically.*

- *The speech is interrupted by the entrance of Macbeth. Decide how she might continue if he did not arrive when he does and whether she has more to say.*

WHERE ELSE TO LOOK ☞ *Joan la Pucelle (Henry VI, Part One, p. 74) and Queen Margaret (Henry VI, Part Three, p. 80) are other women prepared to do men's work.*

Lady Macbeth

" The raven himself is hoarse
That croaks the fatal entrance of Duncan
Under my battlements. Come, you spirits
That tend on mortal thoughts,* unsex me here,
And fill me from the crown to the toe top-full
Of direst cruelty. Make thick my blood,
Stop up th'access and passage to remorse,
That no compunctious* visitings of nature
Shake my fell purpose, nor keep peace between
Th'effect and it. Come to my woman's breasts,
And take my milk for gall,* you murdering ministers,
Wherever in your sightless substances
You wait on nature's mischief. Come, thick night,
And pall* thee in the dunnest smoke of hell,
That my keen knife see not the wound it makes,
Nor heaven peep through the blanket of the dark,
To cry, 'Hold, hold!' **"**

(Act 1, scene 5, lines 38–54)

GLOSSARY

tend on mortal thoughts – pay heed to human wishes
compunctious – remorseful
gall – bile, something bitter
pall – cover

Macbeth

WHO ☞ *Lady Macduff.*

WHERE ☞ *The Macduffs' castle in Fife.*

WHO ELSE IS THERE ☞ *Her young son, and Ross, a nobleman.*

WHAT IS HAPPENING ☞ *Lady Macduff's husband has left Scotland for England to join the rebellion against King Macbeth. She fears for the lives of herself and her children whom Macduff has left behind.*

WHAT TO THINK ABOUT ☞

- *Lady Macduff questions her husband's behaviour. She can be angry, amazed, confused, lonely, frightened at different times in the speech.*
- *Then she wonders what to do for herself and the focus moves from her husband to the plight of herself and her children.*
- *She realises that doing evil is often thought praiseworthy ('laudable') and so to plead innocence will do her no good.*
- *Decide how bleak, quiet and abandoned she must feel at the end of the speech.*
- *Think about the way in which the idea of 'flight' runs through Lady Macduff's words.*

WHERE ELSE TO LOOK ☞ *Another wife fearing death is Imogen (Cymbeline, p. 120). Other wives feeling abandoned – or worse – by their husbands are Lady Anne (Richard III, p. 82) and Queen Katharine (Henry VIII, p. 84).*

Lady Macduff

" What had he done, to make him fly the land?
His flight was madness. When our actions do not,
Our fears do make us traitors.
Wisdom? To leave his wife, to leave his babes,
His mansion and his titles,* in a place
From whence himself does fly? He loves us not,
He wants the natural touch;* for the poor wren,
The most diminutive of birds, will fight,
Her young ones in her nest, against the owl.
All is the fear, and nothing is the love;
As little is the wisdom, where the flight
So runs against all reason.
                              Whither should I fly?
I have done no harm. But I remember now
I am in this earthly world, where to do harm
Is often laudable, to do good sometime
Accounted dangerous folly. Why then, alas,
Do I put up that womanly defence,
To say I have done no harm? **"**

(*Act 4, scene 2, lines 1–77, with some cuts*)

GLOSSARY

his mansion and his titles – both his home and his entitlement to it
wants the natural touch – lacks basic instinct

Hamlet

WHO ☞   *Ophelia, Prince Hamlet's girlfriend.*

WHERE ☞   *A room in the royal castle of Elsinore, Denmark.*

WHO ELSE IS THERE ☞   *Ophelia's father, Polonius, and King Claudius are hiding behind a curtain having been eavesdropping on her meeting with Hamlet which has just ended with Hamlet berating her before leaving.*

WHAT IS HAPPENING ☞   *Hamlet's violent outburst against her has left Ophelia distraught at what has happened to the man she loves.*

WHAT TO THINK ABOUT ☞

- *Hamlet has just behaved abusively to Ophelia. Perhaps she is crying or weeping, having difficulty knowing what to think and how to express her thoughts.*

- *She remembers all that she loves about him. Make each of these qualities individual.*

- *Notice the repetition of 'quite', and how it might affect delivery of the line.*

- *Ophelia thinks about Hamlet before she thinks about herself.*

- *Decide how his behaviour to her has affected her love for him.*

- *Decide whether she remembers that her father and the King are still in hiding.*

- *Notice the final rhyming couplet. She has nothing left to say and is exhausted.*

WHERE ELSE TO LOOK ☞   *Desdemona (Othello, p. 112) is also distressed by the behaviour of the man she loves.*

Ophelia

" O, what a noble mind is here o'erthrown!
The courtier's, soldier's, scholar's, eye, tongue, sword,
Th'expectancy and rose* of the fair state,
The glass* of fashion, and the mould of form,*
Th'observ'd of all observers – quite, quite down!
And I, of ladies most deject and wretched,
That suck'd the honey of his music vows,
Now see that noble and most sovereign reason
Like sweet bells jangled, out of tune and harsh;
That unmatch'd form and feature of blown youth
Blasted with ecstasy.* O, woe is me,
T'have seen what I have seen, see what I see. **"**

(Act 3, scene 1, lines 159–70)

GLOSSARY

expectancy and rose – vary expectation
glass – looking-glass, mirror
mould of form – model of behaviour
blasted with ecstasy – blighted with madness

King Lear

WHO ☞ *Goneril, the eldest of King Lear's three daughters, married to the Duke of Albany.*

WHERE ☞ *A hall in the palace of the Duke of Albany in ancient Britain.*

WHO ELSE IS THERE ☞ *Her father, Lear, with his Fool.*

WHAT IS HAPPENING ☞ *Lear has divided up his kingdom between his daughters. Now without power, Lear has become a burden to his daughters and Goneril tells him she will no longer tolerate the disruptive behaviour of him and his men.*

WHAT TO THINK ABOUT ☞

- *Make decisions about Goneril's attitude to her father. She is scheming and ambitious and now has power. Think about the history of this father/daughter relationship.*

- *Note that she calls him 'Sir', not father.*

- *Have a picture in your head of the behaviour of Lear and his followers that is causing such upset.*

- *Decide whether everything Goneril says is true or whether she is exaggerating so as to exercise her new power over her father.*

- *Goneril ends by talking of herself in the third person (as 'her') and says that she 'will take the thing she begs' if Lear does not do what she asks.*

WHERE ELSE TO LOOK ☞ *Other imperious women of rank include Lady Constance (King John, p. 64) and Queen Margaret (Henry VI, Part Three, p. 80). Miranda (The Tempest, p. 20) also chides her father.*

Goneril

❝ Not only, sir, this your all-licens'd fool,
But other of your insolent retinue

Do hourly carp* and quarrel, breaking forth
In rank and not-to-be endurèd riots. Sir,
I had thought by making this well known unto you
To have found a safe redress, but now grow fearful
By what yourself too late have spoke and done,
That you protect this course, and put it on
By your allowance; which if you should, the fault
Would not scape censure, nor the redresses sleep,
Which in the tender of a wholesome weal*
Might in their working do you that offence
Which else were shame, that then necessity
Will call discreet proceeding.
This admiration, sir, is much o'th' savour
Of other your new pranks. I do beseech you
To understand my purposes aright:
As you are old and reverend, should be wise.
Here do you keep a hundred knights and squires,
Men so disorder'd, so debosh'd* and bold,
That this our court, infected with their manners,
Shows like a riotous inn. Epicurism* and lust
Make it more like a tavern or a brothel
Than a grac'd palace. The shame itself doth speak
For instant remedy. Be then desir'd
By her, that else will take the thing she begs,
A little to disquantity* your train,
And the remainders that shall still depend
To be such men as may besort* your age,
Which know themselves and you. **99**

(*Act 1, scene 4, lines 223–75, with some cuts*)

GLOSSARY

carp – moan
weal – community
debosh'd – debauched
Epicurism – gluttony
disquantity – reduce
besort – suit

Othello

WHO ☞ *Desdemona, married to Othello, a noble Moor in the service of the Venetian State.*

WHERE ☞ *The military garrison in Cyprus where Othello is commander and Iago his 'ensign' or aide. Perhaps contemporaneous with Shakespeare.*

WHO ELSE IS THERE ☞ *Iago and his wife Emilia.*

WHAT IS HAPPENING ☞ *Believing her to have been unfaithful, Desdemona's husband Othello has called her a whore of Venice. She asks Iago what she can do to win back Othello's love.*

WHAT TO THINK ABOUT ☞

- *Desdemona turns to Iago for help but then kneels. What follows may be as much a prayer and a moment of reflection as it is a speech to those with her.*

- *She is completely bewildered by Othello's behaviour and is trying to make sense of it.*

- *She perhaps thinks over their relationship and her behaviour to see if there is anything she can remember to account for Othello's accusations.*

- *Desdemona says that she cannot say the word 'whore', so decide how painful and difficult is it for the word to come out of her mouth and what she thinks once she has said it.*

WHERE ELSE TO LOOK ☞ *Ophelia (Hamlet, p. 108) too is heartbroken by the behaviour of the man she loves.*

Desdemona

" Alas Iago,
What shall I do to win my lord again?
Good friend, go to him, for, by this light of heaven,
I know not how I lost him. Here I kneel.
If e'er my will did trespass 'gainst his love,
Either in discourse of thought or actual deed,
Or that mine eyes, mine ears, or any sense
Delighted them* in any other form,
Or that I do not yet, and ever did,
And ever will – though he do shake me off
To beggarly divorcement – love him dearly,
Comfort forswear me!* Unkindness may do much,
And his unkindness may defeat my life,
But never taint my love. I cannot say 'whore':
It does abhor* me now I speak the word;
To do the act that might the addition earn
Not the world's mass of vanity could make me. **"**

(*Act 4, scene 2, lines 153–69*)

GLOSSARY

Delighted them – took pleasure
Comfort forswear me! – may happiness abandon me!
abhor – disgust

Othello

WHO ☞ *Emilia, wife of Iago, a villainous 'ensign' or aide to Othello, a noble Moor in the service of the Venetian State.*

WHERE ☞ *The military garrison in Cyprus, perhaps contemporaneous with Shakespeare.*

WHO ELSE IS THERE ☞ *Desdemona, Othello's wife.*

WHAT IS HAPPENING ☞ *Desdemona, Othello's wife, has been hurt and confused by Othello's treatment of her. Emilia gives her advice about the behaviour of husbands.*

WHAT TO THINK ABOUT ☞

- *Decide what personal experiences Emilia draws on in this speech.*
- *Perhaps when she says 'say they strike us' it is because she has been struck by Iago.*
- *Maybe these thoughts are ones she has not been able to express before.*
- *Decide if she herself has been unfaithful or been tempted to be, how much she loves Iago and how their relationship has altered with time.*
- *Notice the final rhyming couplet and think how it might be used as a strong finish.*

WHERE ELSE TO LOOK ☞ *Lady Anne (Richard III, p. 82) is talking to other women about her husband. The Countess (All's Well That Ends Well, p. 48) is another older woman talking to a younger.*

Emilia

66 But I do think it is their husbands' faults
If wives do fall.* Say that they slack their duties
And pour our treasures into foreign laps,
Or else break out in peevish jealousies,
Throwing restraint upon us; or say they strike us,
Or scant our former having* in despite –
Why, we have galls,* and though we have some grace,
Yet have we some revenge. Let husbands know
Their wives have sense like them: they see and smell,
And have their palates both for sweet and sour,
As husbands have. What is it that they do
When they change us for others? Is it sport?
I think it is. And doth affection* breed it?
I think it doth. Is't frailty that thus errs?
It is so too. And have not we affections,
Desires for sport, and frailty, as men have?
Then let them use us well: else let them know,
The ills we do, their ills instruct us so. 99

(*Act 4, scene 3, lines 89–106*)

GLOSSARY

fall – succumb to temptation
scant our former having – reduce what they used to give us
galls – tempers
affection – lust

Antony and Cleopatra

WHO ☞   *Cleopatra, Queen of Egypt.*

WHERE ☞   *A room in her palace in Egypt, c. 30 BC.*

WHO ELSE IS THERE ☞   *Cleopatra's attendants: Charmian, Iras and the eunuch Mardian.*

WHAT IS HAPPENING ☞   *Cleopatra wonders aloud to her maid Charmian where her lover Antony might be now. She thinks back to two previous powerful men who have loved her, Julius Caesar and Gnaeus Pompey.*

WHAT TO THINK ABOUT ☞

- *This is an intimate female scene, with the Queen left alone with her attendants.*

- *Enjoy the indulgence and overt sexuality of the speech.*

- *Cleopatra wishes she could be the horse under Antony. Decide what this could say about their sexual relationship and how it might be reflected in the physicality of the scene.*

- *Make Antony alive as Cleopatra speaks his words.*

- *Cleopatra exults in the seductive power of her body 'black, / And wrinkled deep in time'.*

WHERE ELSE TO LOOK ☞   *Other speeches filled with erotic desire come from Tamora (Titus Andronicus, p. 94) and Juliet (Romeo and Juliet, p. 100).*

Cleopatra

❝ O Charmian,
Where think'st thou he is now? Stands he, or sits he?
Or does he walk? Or is he on his horse?
O happy horse to bear the weight of Antony!
Do bravely, horse, for wot'st thou* whom thou mov'st?
The demi-Atlas of this earth, the arm
And burgonet* of men. He's speaking now,
Or murmuring 'Where's my serpent of old Nile?'
(For so he calls me). Now I feed myself
With most delicious poison. Think on me
That am with Phoebus'* amorous pinches black,
And wrinkled deep in time. Broad-fronted Caesar,
When thou wast here above the ground, I was
A morsel for a monarch: and great Pompey*
Would stand and make his eyes grow in my brow,
There would he anchor his aspect,* and die
With looking on his life. **❞**

(Act 1, scene 5, lines 18–34)

GLOSSARY

wot'st thou – do you know
burgonet – helmet
Phoebus – the personification of the sun (pronounced '*Fee-bus*')
aspect – gaze

Antony and Cleopatra

WHO ☞ *Cleopatra, Queen of Egypt.*

WHERE ☞ *A monument in her palace in Egypt, c. 30* BC.

WHO ELSE IS THERE ☞ *Cleopatra's attendants: Charmian and Iras and her maids.*

WHAT IS HAPPENING ☞ *The war with Octavius Caesar being lost and her lover Antony having just killed himself, Cleopatra prepares herself for death.*

WHAT TO THINK ABOUT ☞

- *Antony has only just died, having killed himself out of honour after losing the war. His body is still warm beside Cleopatra.*
- *The great Queen and lover realises that she is just a woman like any other.*
- *The journey of the speech is from Cleopatra being reduced to being a woman at the mercy of the same passions as any other, to deciding to kill herself in a way worthy of her status 'after the high Roman fashion'. Allow time for that journey to take place.*
- *She asks herself whether it is a sin to commit suicide.*
- *She talks to her attendants but gets no response from them.*
- *She then decides to kill herself.*
- *The speech can end grandly with the strong rhyming couplet just as it began simply.*

WHERE ELSE TO LOOK ☞ *There is a sense of having lost everything in Hermione's speech (The Winter's Tale, p. 56).*

Cleopatra

❝ No more, but e'en* a woman, and commanded
By such poor passion, as the maid that milks
And does the meanest chares.* It were for me
To throw my sceptre at the injurious gods,
To tell them that this world did equal theirs,
Till they had stol'n our jewel. All's but naught.
Patience is sottish,* and impatience does
Become a dog that's mad. Then is it sin,
To rush into the secret house of death,
Ere death dare come to us? How do you, women?
What, what, good cheer! Why, how now, Charmian?
My noble girls! Ah, women, women! Look,
Our lamp is spent, it's out. Good sirs, take heart,
We'll bury him. And then, what's brave, what's noble,
Let's do't after the high Roman fashion,*
And make death proud to take us. Come, away,
This case of that huge spirit now is cold.
Ah, women, women! Come, we have no friend
But resolution, and the briefest end. **❞**

(*Act 4, scene 15, lines 75–93*)

GLOSSARY

e'en – just
chares – chores
sottish – stupid
Let's do't after the high Roman fashion – commit suicide, which the
    Romans believed to be a noble way to die.

Cymbeline

WHO ☞   *Imogen, daughter of Cymbeline, King of Britain.*

WHERE ☞   *In Wales, by a cave, in ancient Britain.*

WHO ELSE IS THERE ☞   *Imogen is alone.*

WHAT IS HAPPENING ☞   *Imogen has travelled all the way to the far western coast of Wales in search of her husband, Posthumus, who has been banished. Posthumus's servant Pisanio has pointed out Milford Haven to her and that is where she is headed. She has disguised herself as a boy for safety.*

WHAT TO THINK ABOUT ☞

- *This is a wild and lonely setting and Imogen has travelled a huge distance. Her destination still seems far away.*

- *Her love is giving her the strength to keep going. Every time she weakens it is the thought of Posthumous that revives her.*

- *She seeks shelter. Work out the geography of the setting.*

- *Decide, when she finds the cave, how scared she is about what or who might be inside it and how daring it is to enter the cave.*

- *Decide how loudly she shouts. Each 'hoa' can be different from the other.*

WHERE ELSE TO LOOK ☞   *Hermia too is lost and has to find her way (A Midsummer Night's Dream, p. 30). Viola has had to dress in male clothes for her own protection (Twelfth Night, p. 52).*

Imogen

❝ I see a man's life is a tedious one.
I have tir'd myself,* and for two nights together
Have made the ground my bed. I should be sick,
But that my resolution helps me. Milford,
When from the mountain-top Pisanio show'd thee,
Thou wast within a ken.* O Jove, I think
Foundations fly the wretched: such, I mean,
Where they should be reliev'd.* Two beggars told me,
I could not miss my way. Will poor folks lie,
That have afflictions on them, knowing 'tis
A punishment, or trial? Yes; no wonder,
When rich ones scarce tell true. To lapse in fullness
Is sorer than to lie for need. And falsehood
Is worse in kings than beggars. My dear lord,
Thou art one o' the false ones. Now I think on thee,
My hunger's gone; but even before, I was
At point to sink, for food. But what is this?
Here is a path to't: 'tis some savage hold:
I were best not call; I dare not call: yet famine
Ere clean it o'erthrow nature, makes it valiant.
Plenty and peace breeds cowards. Hardness ever
Of hardiness is mother. Hoa? Who's here?
If anything that's civil, speak; if savage,
Take or lend. Hoa? No answer? Then I'll enter.
Best draw my sword; and if mine enemy
But fear the sword like me, he'll scarcely look on't.
Such a foe, good heavens! **❞**

(Act 3, scene 6, lines 1–27)

GLOSSARY

tir'd myself – exhausted myself
within a ken – within sight
foundations fly the wretched . . . where they should be reliev'd – strength
    abandons the wretched when they should be helped

The Two Noble Kinsmen

WHO ☞ *The Jailer's Daughter.*

WHERE ☞ *A prison in Athens, in ancient Greece,*

WHO ELSE IS THERE ☞ *The Jailer's Daughter is alone.*

WHAT IS HAPPENING ☞ *Thebes is at war with Athens. Two noblemen from Thebes, the cousins Arcite and Palamon, have been imprisoned in an Athenian jail. The Jailer's Daughter (who remains nameless throughout the play) has fallen in love with Palamon.*

WHAT TO THINK ABOUT ☞

- *The Daughter's love is young, sexual and almost obsessive. She will later go mad because her love is not requited. Find the intensity of this passion.*

- *Follow her falling in love as she recounts it, from seeing Palamon, to pitying him and then to loving him.*

- *Enjoy the thrice repeated 'lov'd him'.*

- *A new thought then enters her head and she wonders why she did not fall in love with the other prisoner instead.*

- *She talks of Palamon's singing and his 'fair spoken' voice. She might try to imitate that voice as she recalls his talking to her.*

- *Picture what it was like to be kissed by Palamon and what it might be like to recall that kiss.*

WHERE ELSE TO LOOK ☞ *Also young and in love in their different ways are Juliet (Romeo and Juliet, pp. 98 and 100) and Helena (All's Well That Ends Well, p. 46).*

The Jailer's Daughter

❝ Why should I love this gentleman? 'Tis odds
He never will affect* me. I am base,
My father the mean keeper of his prison,

And he a prince. To marry him is hopeless;
To be his whore is witless. Out upon't,
What pushes are we wenches driven to,
When fifteen once has found us.* First, I saw him.
I, seeing, thought he was a goodly man.
He has as much to please a woman in him,
If he please to bestow it so, as ever
These eyes yet look'd on. Next, I pitied him,
And so would any young wench, o' my conscience,
That ever dream'd, or vow'd her maidenhead
To a young handsome man. Then I lov'd him,
Extremely lov'd him, infinitely lov'd him.
And yet he had a cousin, fair as he too.
But in my heart was Palamon, and there,
Lord, what a coil he keeps.* To hear him
Sing in an evening, what a heaven it is!
And yet his songs are sad ones. Fairer spoken
Was never gentleman. When I come in
To bring him water in a morning, first
He bows his noble body, then salutes me, thus:
'Fair, gentle maid, good morrow; may thy goodness
Get thee a happy husband.' Once he kiss'd me.
I lov'd my lips the better ten days after.
Would he would do so ev'ry day! He grieves much,
And me as much to see his misery.
What should I do, to make him know I love him?
For I would fain enjoy him. Say I ventur'd
To set him free? What says the law then? Thus much
For law, or kindred! I will do it,
And this night, or tomorrow, he shall love me. **99**

(*Act 2, scene 4, lines 1–33*)

GLOSSARY

affect – love
When fifteen once has found us – once we reach the age of puberty
what a coil he keeps – what a turmoil he makes